# Take the U
# Out of Clutter

# Take the U Out of Clutter

### THE LAST CLUTTER BOOK
### YOU'LL EVER NEED

## Mark Brunetz *and*
## Carmen Renee Berry

BERKLEY BOOKS, NEW YORK

**THE BERKLEY PUBLISHING GROUP**
**Published by the Penguin Group**
**Penguin Group (USA) Inc.**
**375 Hudson Street, New York, New York 10014, USA**
Penguin Group (Canada), 90 Eglinton Avenue East, Suite 700, Toronto, Ontario M4P 2Y3, Canada
(a division of Pearson Penguin Canada Inc.)
Penguin Books Ltd., 80 Strand, London WC2R 0RL, England
Penguin Group Ireland, 25 St. Stephen's Green, Dublin 2, Ireland (a division of Penguin Books Ltd.)
Penguin Group (Australia), 250 Camberwell Road, Camberwell, Victoria 3124, Australia
(a division of Pearson Australia Group Pty. Ltd.)
Penguin Books India Pvt. Ltd., 11 Community Centre, Panchsheel Park, New Delhi—110 017, India
Penguin Group (NZ), 67 Apollo Drive, Rosedale, North Shore, 0632, New Zealand
(a division of Pearson New Zealand Ltd.)
Penguin Books (South Africa) (Pty.) Ltd., 24 Sturdee Avenue, Rosebank, Johannesburg 2196,
South Africa
Penguin Books Ltd., Registered Offices: 80 Strand, London WC2R 0RL, England

The publisher does not have any control over and does not assume any responsibility for author or third-party websites or their content.

Copyright © 2010 Mark Brunetz and Carmen Renee Berry
Cover design by Pyrographx and George Long
Cover photo of author by Steve Anderson
Cover photo of room by Chris Ameruoso
Book design by Tiffany Estreicher

PRINTING HISTORY
Berkley trade paperback edition / May 2010

Library of Congress Cataloging-in-Publication Data

Brunetz, Mark.
    Take the U out of clutter / Mark Brunetz and Carmen Renee Berry.—1st ed.
        p. cm.
    ISBN 978-0-425-23409-9
    1. House cleaning.    I. Berry, Carmen Renee.    II. Title.
    TX324.B78 2010
    648—dc22                                                2009050685

PRINTED IN THE UNITED STATES OF AMERICA

10   9   8   7   6   5   4   3   2   1

*To my mom, Caroline Singer, for sharing her remarkable talent
and infinite wisdom since the day I arrived on this planet.
You are with me every step of the way.*
—*Mark Brunetz*


*To my mom, Mary Ellen Berry, who daily demonstrates what it
means to love through all kinds of circumstances. You are my hero.*
—*Carmen Renee Berry*

# ACKNOWLEDGMENTS

From Mark:

To all of my professional colleagues who contributed so poignantly to my journey over the past decade, in particular, the cast and crew of *Clean House* including Niecy Nash, Trish Suhr, and Matt Iseman, thank you for championing my work both on and off camera. To my colleagues at the Style Network, thank you for providing me with a platform in which to change lives. And to the homeowners and clients who opened their homes and their hearts and became my friends along the way, you made all the difference in the world.

To my business partner Lia Brandligt at Design*and*Decorate.com, my assistant Joel Sturdivant, Cameron Kadison at the Paradigm Agency, and above all, John Stellar and Kate-Romero Stellar at Stellar Communications, thank you for your unwavering contribution to the big picture. To my lovely co-author Carmen Renee Berry, bless you for seeing beyond the clutter and collaborating on something very special here. And to Denise Silvestro and Meredith Giordan at the Penguin Group and Kathryn Helmers at Creative Trust, Inc., a sincere thanks for your partnership in bringing this message to the world.

To my kindred spirit, Donna Marie Kent, whose love, enthusiasm and artistry inspire me on a daily basis and to my many dear friends including John Zaffarano, Tom Davila, and Lillian Dean, thank you for granting me the freedom to be me. It's a gift that keeps on giving.

To my family, thank you for always indulging me with curiosity and kindness. And to the love of my life, Eduardo Flores, my deepest gratitude for your love and support over the past eleven years. You are the living expression of all that is blissful in the world. You are *my* treasure.

From Carmen:

My close friends and family know what it's like when I'm possessed with a writing project—how I wander around preoccupied with the manuscript in my mind, unaware of those around me. I want to thank all of you for loving me anyway—even though most of you rolled your eyes when I told you I was writing a book on clutter. You've seen my garage . . . Thanks to the faithful Colleen Sutton, Pat Luehrs, Cathy Smith, Bob Parsons, Joel Miller and Denise Blair. To those who share my love for Nepal—Mike Platter, Joanne Feldmeth, Lindsay Feldmeth, Joseph Rubio, and Rodney Burke.

My journey with clutter has not been an easy one—especially for Marianne Croonquist who schlepped my stuff from house to house while I was learning how to "let go." Thank you, Marianne. The mention of clutter demands a special thanks to Ricky Stewart who has organized and reorganized my garage more times that either of us can remember, and whose joyful encouragement has meant so much to me and my mother. I cannot express how grateful I am to our landlady, Shirley Muse, who welcomed us into a beautiful home in spite of the fact that we had a "few" cats. Every time I look out at the lake, I know God has loved me through you.

To the extraordinary Carolyn Rafferty who has given so generously of her time and energy through numerous adventures. You made this book possible by being a great Auntie to my daughter, Jenee.

I thank Kathryn Helmers, my long-time agent and friend, for sharing of her creativity, encouragement and finding just the right publisher for this project. Special thanks to Denise Silvestro and Meredith Giordan of Penguin for helping us birth something wonderful.

Lastly, I want to thank Mark Brunetz for his generosity, integrity and creativity that seem to know no limits. It has truly been a delight of immeasurable proportions working with you.

# Contents

PART THREE

# Clear the Clutter from the Inside Out

Part One

# You Make the Meaning

# 1

# Let's Be Partners

Don't buy another organizer bin! Don't plan another yard sale! Don't call a local charity to pick up more donations! In fact, don't do anything but get a cup of tea and sit with us for a little while.

Our approach is different from any other. We will be the first to admit that we do not know how you should live your life or organize your home. But we promise you won't be made to feel like you have a psychological problem that needs to be fixed. And since we're fairly certain that you don't need a huge "to-do" list—just something else to feel guilty about—we won't give you 10 or 50 or 1,000 cleaning "tips." Like you, we want to spend less time cleaning and organizing our homes, not more.

Instead, we put the power to create your home environment into *your* hands. We want to ignite your passion for living well, and inspire you to act intentionally, regardless of circumstances. The missing ingredient for creating and maintaining a clutter-free home is self-motivation, and unlimited access to it at all times.

We suspect that this isn't the first book you've bought on how to clear away the clutter. And your house is still full of this, that, and the other thing, right? You're not alone. There are enough people who desire clean, clutter-free homes to support an entire industry—the clutter control and organizational products business! This is a relatively new phenomenon that has arisen over the last thirty years. Many books have been written, many television shows produced, many experts are available for hire for the purpose of telling you how to get organized.

Like many others, you may have a favorite TV show on decluttering that you watch in search of inspiration and cleaning tips. Perhaps you scour the Internet for websites for additional information, hoping that you'll find the perfect scheme. Armed with the latest book or approach to home organization you take off to Home Depot or the Container Store to get the items needed for your new reorganization plan. *This time is going to work*, you promise yourself.

Energized by the vision of an orderly garage or family room, you may purchase the latest system of shelving units or color-coordinated plastic bins. After standing in long lines to pay for your new system, you lug it all into your house. Phew! You're probably tired from all that shopping, but nevertheless, continue your intention of organizational success.

You start installing the new system, but it isn't long before you lose steam. You are distracted by something that seems much more important, like paying bills, watching TV, meeting up with friends, completing the work you brought home, spending time with your children, petting your cat. There are a lot of activities vying for your attention, some of which might actually be important. But when these activities call, you step away for a moment and the moment becomes an hour, the hour becomes a day, the day becomes a week.

Then one day, you trip over the new organizational system and that old familiar sense of defeat creeps into your heart once again. The enormity of the task weighs down on you until you slow to a complete stop. You may sit down to rest on your new organizer bins (at least they're good for something!). Your head aches, your back spasms, or maybe your stomach cramps. Your home is in more disarray with the added organizing books and products you recently purchased strewn about. Instead of helping, they add to the clutter—they are a physical manifestation of the problem itself. Another dissatisfying attempt and more clutter to boot.

Sound familiar? Many people start out with the best of intentions, but somehow get mired down and feel like failures, once again. That's how we felt when we couldn't get anywhere with our piles of stuff. We've all heard the saying, "the definition of insanity is doing the same thing over and over and expecting a different result." In a nutshell, that defines what we used to do: Buy more self-help books and organizing systems in the hopes that one of them will work out. But today, we come at this problem from a completely different direction. This time you won't do the same thing over again. It's time to stop the insanity.

# Clutter as a Catalyst for Positive Change

Now, you might not think that you have the ability to clean up the clutter in your home. After all, you've tried, or at least thought about it, many times. But by the time you finish this book, you will be amazed at how quickly you can get things in order, without all the distractions, stress, and distress you've had in the past. It will actually be easy.

How can we make such a claim? Why do we have faith in our process? Because it was developed to overcome our own challenges with clutter, and has since assisted thousands of other people to produce similar sustainable results. That's right, despite who we now are in our professional lives—a TV host for a top-rated design and organizational show and a practicing stress management consultant and best-selling author—we, too, had clutter, tons of it. At the time, we couldn't remedy our own situations. The amount of effort it took to navigate day-to-day and year-to-year became increasingly overwhelming. We were much like the "cobbler's son" who had no shoes; so-called experts who couldn't successfully confront our own cluttered lives. In fact, it was embarrassing to face the fact that we did not have all of the answers. Only in the end did we realize the path we were taking did not end up where we wanted to go. We knew we needed a completely different direction to arrive at our desired destination.

Previously, we approached clutter from the "outside in" by seeing the clutter, itself, as the source of our problems. We said to ourselves, "If I could just get the right system I'd be fine." Between the two of us, we probably tried just about every approach on the market. Results? Feeling badly about ourselves and frustrated that nothing "worked" for either of us.

Stymied and stumped by what to try next, we confided in each other about our failures—obviously other people could master their spaces, but neither of us could. We both admitted procrastinating when it came to cleaning up clutter. We always seemed to have energy for the activities and people we loved, but going through the pile of clothing on the bottom of the closet? Not enough motivation to actually succeed.

We thought we were merely commiserating about our failures. But then we discovered that the act of storytelling became the catalyst for the positive change we had been looking for all along. We accidentally stumbled onto the most powerful change agent in the world: We created lasting change in our *exterior* spaces by creating lasting change in our *interior* worlds. Our ability to deal effectively with the clutter that was strewn around our homes was directly linked with our personal stories, and the degree to which these stories empowered or disempowered us.

> *We created lasting change in our exterior spaces by creating lasting change in our interior worlds.*

This realization completely transformed the way we view clutter. We no longer saw clutter as the culprit, but actually as the catalyst of deeper personal exploration, healing, and growth. Rather than a source of frustration, clutter became a blessing of sorts—a legitimate means to address the unfinished business in our relationships, increase our spiritual discernment, and awaken us to the true purpose for our lives. This dynamic is the basis for the title of our book, *Take the U Out of Clutter*. By making a distinction between ourselves, as human beings, and the clutter in our homes, as exterior objects, we were finally empowered to create order and opportunity in our lives.

## The Inner "U"

We all have inner space that only we can inhabit. You, and only you, reside in your inner space. Your partner doesn't live there, nor your boss or your mother. It is there, in quietness and tranquility, that the truth about your life is revealed to you. When you remove yourself from the clatter, clamor, and clutter of your exterior life, you come into contact with who you are and the possibilities of who you can become. We call this self-awareness the Inner "U."

When we travel a meaningful path that focuses on the true self, what is discovered can never be taken away. Things in our outer spaces can be removed but who we are on the inside cannot. The true self exists outside of time and cannot be shaped by external pressures or demands. When we worked from the "inside out," beginning in our interior space rather than from our exterior clutter, we were able to see that our things don't define us. Our value was not found in the piece of real estate in which we lived or in the clothes we wore or in any other thing we owned. In the process, we identified three aspects of inner work:

1. *Calmness:* The interior world is a sanctuary from the noisy demands of the exterior world. Body awareness is the doorway to the stillness that always exists in our inner space. It is impossible to be in contact with the interior and be out of touch with our bodies. A simple action, like taking a deep breath, takes you inward to a tranquil world you always possess.

2. *Clarity:* Surrounded by peace and protected from the noisy clatter of daily life, we are able to see the world from a place of being and purpose, not circumstances. New ideas arise, creativity thrives, and solutions to problems present themselves in this state of mind.

3. *Courage:* We experience a fearlessness that comes from being authentic. We are able to deal with anything when we know, from the center of our being, what is right for us. Knowing that the answer to "Why?" is "Because this is authentically you" gives us a determination and confidence unavailable when we're trying to please other people or earn our worth through exterior means.

We could not get organized from the outside in. It simply did not work. The only successful starting point for truly getting organized is within. Everything else is a shortcut and there really are no shortcuts in life, just sidetracks. Looking back, we wish we could say the journey was simple and painless, but it wasn't. However, if we had to do it all over again, we would. In this case, the proverbial "ends justify the means" truly holds water. We developed a foolproof plan that has not only stood the test of time with our clients, but one that is simple and straightforward, and—above all—grounded in who you are as a human being. We have confidence in this process because it is rooted, not in our expertise, but in your interior and authentic self. We'd like to be your tour guides on a journey that will lead you to the goal you desire. It starts with telling our stories.

MARK:

*Growing up on the east side of Cleveland, in Willoughby, Ohio, I spent a big part of my childhood with my grandparents. They had a beautiful split-level house on Lake Shore Boulevard that my grandfather hand-built, like many others he had constructed throughout his career as a builder. Every afternoon after grade school, my brother and I would go to their house and spend time with them until my mom picked us up after work.*

*One of the things I remember most about those afternoons was Grandmother's love of playing the organ. My grandmother would sit at the organ and play song after song, most of which were composed during wartime, so they seemed to have a sense of melancholy about them. I would sit and listen to her play for hours on end. It reminded me of something I vaguely remember as an infant. It was later in life that I learned that most of my early childhood before the age of three was spent listening to my great-grandmother playing the piano.*

*Grammy's Hammond organ sat on one side of the living room. Surrounding it were beautiful furnishings, including a nineteenth-century French music cabinet that housed all of my great-*

grandmother's sheet music. Many of my ancestors played music professionally, and my entire family was musically inclined. My mother played clarinet as a child and I played the trumpet in a youth orchestra by age thirteen. Needless to say, music in the home was a very important part of my childhood. Music was our way of staying connected as a family—through music, we felt that we belonged to one another. Music was my connection to my family and in a way, the organ and my great-grandmother's music cabinet were symbols of that bond.

My mother was an interior designer by trade, with a love of fine antiques. This, coupled with her impeccable skill in interior design, gave me the opportunity to grow up in some of the most beautifully decorated spaces I've ever seen, even to this day. It also taught me, among many other things, that family heirlooms are signs of success and that they are to be preserved at all cost.

During my high school years, my family relocated to North Carolina and one day during my senior year I remember winning a fifty dollar gift certificate at a local mall where I could purchase anything I wanted. At the time, my heart was set on buying my first pair of Levi's but after wandering store to store, I ended up buying a hand-carved wooden duck. It reminded me of the handmade decoy ducks my great-grandfather had sitting in his living room in his cottage house in the Harbor on Lake Eric. As crazy as it sounds, I named the duck Howie. It was while writing this book some thirty years later that I realized I actually named it after my great-grandfather, Howard Poor.

After graduating from high school, I attended college in Greenville, North Carolina. My first place was an apartment off-campus, and from there, I moved into several houses with roommates. I remember leaving for school with an entire U-Haul truck full of beautiful furnishings

*my mom had given me. Many were from the family, others were fur-*
*nishings she had purchased during the many remodels she undertook*
*at our house in Raleigh. I'm confident I was the only freshman who*
*had a completely furnished place replete with a Jacobean dining room*
*table and chairs, a Victorian sideboard, a bamboo shirt trunk, and*
*a collection of antique tennis rackets from the early '40s. Seriously, I*
*had more stuff in my first college place than most of my friends have*
*today. I continued the tradition of preserving "family treasures" and*
*spent all my disposable income on adding to them—bamboo canes,*
*cigar boxes, you name it, I collected it. People would come over and*
*say they thought I was a trust-fund baby. Truth be told, even though I*
*had a partial academic scholarship, I worked my way through college,*
*both undergraduate and graduate school. It just looked like I lived the*
*high life.*

*After graduate school, I accepted my first job as the staff exercise*
*physiologist at the Jane Fonda Workout in Beverly Hills where I would*
*oversee the personal training staff and go on to create several of Jane's*
*workout videos. Without hesitation, I packed every single item from*
*my place in North Carolina and transported them to Los Angeles with*
*plans to move into a small one-bedroom apartment off Melrose Ave-*
*nue. Needless to say, only half of what I brought actually fit into my*
*new place. This is when I first discovered what a storage unit was. For*
*eighty dollars a month, I stored most of what I had brought to L.A.*
*knowing that I could never part with those things as doing so would be*
*like parting with my past, and more important, my family.*

*Over the next fifteen years, I moved from place to place throughout*
*Los Angeles, each new residence slightly larger than the last one. And*
*even though my rent was high and space was still limited, I continued*

*to collect furniture. A man on a mission, I went to flea markets and yard sales on the weekends, also hitting all the antique shops I could find. I quickly amassed a large amount of stuff spending nearly every penny I earned. By now, I was paying two hundred dollars a month for two storage units. At the time, I was earning a salary of $28,500 a year and my rent was upward of $1600 a month. Quick math should have shown me that I had a problem, but I wasn't paying attention.*

*In 2002, my grandmother passed away at the young age of 74. I was heartbroken. I flew back to Cleveland to attend her funeral and be with the rest of the family and my grandfather, who was now frail and barely getting around with the help of a wheelchair. My grandparents had moved to a ranch-style home in Willoughby and managed to relocate everything from their house on the lake into this slightly smaller house. The place was absolutely filled with collectibles and family furnishings. I literally couldn't walk two steps without bumping into something. It was a result of years of accumulating and never parting with anything. Everything was imbued with family meaning and "of value"–or so I was told.*

*As I maneuvered my way through the house, my first instinct was to start identifying things to take back to L.A. with me, things that would remind me of my grandmother and the wonderful times we had together. As I considered the Econolite lamp that mimicked snowfall and mesmerized me as a child or the hundreds of dolls that lined their guest room bed, I realized something awful. This cluttered home with layers upon layers of stuff looked eerily similar to my crowded house on the West Coast and the two storage units that I had been maintaining for the past fifteen years. The similarity was uncanny and overwhelming all at once.*

What had I gotten myself into? *I asked.* Did my grandmother really intend to leave all this stuff behind? *And more important,* is this how she—the person who taught me to never settle for anything less than the best in life—wanted me to live? *They say the apple doesn't fall far from the tree and I was living proof.* Had I inherited my family's clutter gene? *The answers were suddenly obvious, and for the first time, I started seeing things differently. I was so wrapped up in missing my family after moving to the West Coast that the only way I knew how to keep them close was to buy things that reminded me of them. Little did I know, the financial burden of maintaining storage units coupled with my poor use of interior space, prevented me from visiting them or having them stay with me as often as I wanted. The idea of hanging onto stuff became the obstacle that moved me further and further from them.*

*This realization coupled with a deep sense of sadness and loss proved to be one of the most transformational times in my life. I understood then and there, that no matter how much stuff I had from my family and no matter how hard I worked to maintain possession of it, it would never bring my family closer, and in this case, my grandmother back. All I could do was hold the memory of her in my heart. And now, for the first time in my life, I began seeing who and what was really important to me.*

*I arrived back in L.A. and removed everything from my storage unit. I sorted through every box and every container uncovering every last layer of my possessions. I chose only to keep the things that would fit into my current life. I created rules for how I would live my life. I decided to live within my means for the first time because, in my heart, I believed that this is how my grandmother, my mom, and*

# Mark's Definition of Clutter

For me, clutter consists of things that have no personal value to you. As the son of an accomplished interior designer and avid collector of vintage furniture, I came to believe early on that the only things that really mattered in a home were items that were of value in the marketplace. Back then I thought that anything that wasn't of financial value wasn't of value to me as it was either disposable or could easily be replaced. It wasn't a collectible.

It took me some time to realize that collectible things could become clutter like any other item. It didn't matter if they were "of value;" they had no true value to me because I never planned to sell them. On a practical level, I wasn't using these items. They were primarily for me to look at and talk about versus utilizing them as practical pieces. One day, I realized my home was more of a museum than it was a residence.

My desire to collect things, which as I call it caused "collectible clutter," was amplified by the fact that my mom gave me so many of the things she collected. Over time, I discovered that I was living way beyond my financial and spatial means. Space was a commodity in the places I lived and truthfully, I had more things than the space allowed so I had to put things into storage. I became a slave to my collectibles. Every day, I would wake up feeling like there was a ball and chain strapped to my ankle. I spent so much of my time earning an income to maintain these items that were really not serving me on a daily basis. I realized I, too, had clutter. And parting with a collectible seemed to go against the good sense my mom had worked so hard to instill in me. It was an emotional battle and I was losing.

*everyone else who has contributed so unselfishly to my path would have wanted it to be. Above all, it was how I wanted it to be. And as my place became more and more in tune with me, something else magical happened. Each of my siblings decided to live with me in California at one point or another. Even though we always saw each other as often as possible, this marked a new era in my relationships with them. As for my mom, her love and contribution have been unwavering. We continue to share an incredible relationship and now more than ever it centers on sharing quality time and wonderful experiences together.*

*Looking back, it seems that early on I began associating things with memories to the extent that one day, the memories and the things were indistinguishable. I think I truly believed that if I got rid of anything I would lose the memories I treasured. It took a deep loss and an eye-opening moment for me to realize that my memories would always belong to me, and my grandmother would always remain in my thoughts and in my heart.*

*My grandfather passed away a couple of years after my grandmother and naturally I attended his funeral. My mom and her siblings later sorted through my grandparents' home. They had an estate sale and donated the rest of their stuff to charity. Of course, a few treasured items were kept amongst the family. I was not able to be at the sale, but I was at peace with that. Today, several pictures of my grandparents adorn my house. I wear my grandfather's gold signet ring for special occasions and there's always music playing in my home and in my heart. Carried down through my mom, this was my grandparents' true legacy and I am forever grateful for their gift.*

*In dealing with the excess stuff in my home, I had cleared the way for what mattered in my heart and continues to matter most to me—my family, my friends, and myself. On the professional front, I rekindled my love for interior design and launched my interior design firm in Los Angeles in 2001. It's no accident that within a few short years I would find myself on a television show about decluttering and design. And now after seven years working one-on-one with a thousand-plus homeowners, I decided it was time to share this message that enables people to live out their dreams in a way they never dreamed possible. And this is what led me to Carmen.*

## Carmen:

*My relationship with collecting, accumulating, and clutter stretches back to the Great Depression of the 1930s. Both of my parents grew up during this time period—a time of poverty that hit my father's family especially hard. He told me stories of my grandmother baking bread so that he could fill his little red wagon with loaves of bread that he sold for five cents each. My father's attitude was, "Don't throw that away! We might need it someday!"*

*My mother's family was impacted in a different way. Rather than hold on to everything they had, my grandparents spent the little money available on a few items of fine quality. My grandfather was a pastor so church members were continually visiting or coming over for a meal. My grandmother put extra attention on keeping their house neat and tidy, and always displayed their beautiful treasures.*

*After my parents married and I came along, my mother made sure that our house was artistically decorated and my father had his garage for his many projects. My dad never parked a car in the garage—that's not what a garage is for! It's for making go-carts and teeter-totters and electric guitars. I loved the time I spent with my father in his garage helping him build our newest project. We painted, soldered, oiled,* and sawed; we made shortwave radios and electric games as good as any in an arcade. Mom insisted we clean up before we came into the house—but in the garage, it was okay to be messy.

My mother expressed her creativity through home decorating. As a little girl, I watched her paint an elegant mural of Roman columns on our dining room wall. In my room, she painted a fantasy scene of a castle with a princess, amidst lush greenery. My mother taught me how to pick out paint colors for the walls, how to sew draperies, and hang wallpaper. Both of my parents expressed themselves creatively, and I was able to benefit from both of their styles.

As the years passed, my father's garage began to fill up with all of the things we had created, along with his tools and yard-sale finds. I went off to college, and on my visits home, I noticed that the garage was getting fuller and fuller. I had outgrown the shared projects my father and I so enjoyed when I was a child. Then, with all the clutter, I just stopped going into the garage at all.

I obtained a master's degree in social work from the University of Southern California, and worked in the area of child abuse prevention and treatment. Feeling like a grown-up, I bought my first condo, and took on the "decorate the house, store everything else in the garage" mentality I had learned from my parents. I delighted in planning my decorating projects, as well as executing them. I was always able to park my car in the garage, but I rarely threw anything away, and never sold anything. I kept it all. At that time, I had room for it all.

In 1987, my first book, When Helping You Is Hurting Me, was published. I continued to author and coauthor books, traveling extensively around the country to give seminars on the prevention of burnout and stress management techniques. In 1995, a friend of mine and I coauthored Girlfriends, a book that celebrated women's friendships.

*Our work was featured on* Oprah. Girlfriends *shot onto the* New York Times *bestsellers list where it stayed for a year. I accumulated more things and my garage got fuller and fuller.*

*In October of 1997, my father was pruning a tree in the front yard of my parents' home and the limb broke, knocking him to the ground. He sustained a serious head injury, two broken vertebrae, and a broken leg. He was a strong man, and he fought valiantly, but passed away four months later at the age of 71.*

*That was a turning point in my life in so many ways. I experienced intense grief. As an only child, it fell on my shoulders to help my mother manage life without my father. We lived about forty-five minutes apart and she didn't like being in that huge house alone. We both sold our homes and bought condos near each other. My mother wanted just enough furniture to fill her new condo, and was willing to sell everything else.*

*I walked around the house I grew up in, overwhelmed by all of the things my parents had collected during their forty-six years of marriage. They had traveled extensively through Europe and the Far East. After falling in love with Japan, my parents moved there for five years to teach English, bringing back boxes and boxes of mementos and gifts given to them by friends. I wanted my mother to keep the items that meant something to her.*

*As I continued moving from room to room, I saw the hutch that had guarded many a Thanksgiving dinner, the oak secretary desk I loved in the office, my grandmother's upright piano . . . one item after another had meaning for me. I didn't want to give up any of these memories.*

*Then I opened the door into the garage, a place that I had not seen for years, and ran right into a literal wall of clutter—so much stuff that I couldn't get into the room. Over the next few weeks, I dismantled several layers of shelving. My father had built shelves around the walls.*

Once these were filled, he had built more shelves, in the middle of the garage. And then more shelves in between the shelves. And a few more up higher. My dad had created a three-dimensional clutter puzzle, filling the entire garage, wall to wall, back to front, floor to ceiling.

It was a massive effort to clear out and sort through that garage before we could put the house on the market. It was painful. What would I do with manual typewriters or black rotary phones? How could I use outdated electronics? The walls were lined with baby-food jars from my toddler years, now filled with nails, washers, and screws. There were stacks of lumber, 8-track tape players, and things I couldn't even identify. It was agonizingly difficult for me to think of getting rid of any of it, but I had no use for these things

Why was it so hard? Not because these items were important to me, but because I knew all of it—every single thing in that garage— had been important to my dad. I didn't want to demean my father's memory by treating his valued possessions disrespectfully. It felt that treating the contents of his garage like trash was equivalent to treating my father as if he were trash. And he wasn't. He was my father.

We were finally able to sell the family home and my mother moved into her condo. She took the matching furniture and high-quality items—and I got the rest. I must say, this was my choice. I could not bear to part with a large portion of what I saw as my childhood memories. I ended up with a house of mismatched furniture without a decorating theme and a garage bulging with stuff I had no use for. In spite of having no room, I continued to accumulate even more furniture and decorating items in an effort to bring a theme to my home. I kept a narrow strip cleared out in the garage so I could park my car, but otherwise my garage looked just like my father's.

*In the process of selling and buying multiple pieces of real estate properties, I realized that I enjoyed the process. I added "real estate agent" to my resume. I liked helping my clients showcase their homes—by clearing away the extra furnishings and knickknacks. It was a case of "do as I say, but not as I do." I helped other people eliminate excessive clutter that might turn off prospective buyers, while living in a muddled environment myself.*

*For years I had wanted to be a parent. In 2003, I decided to adopt a child. Planning on being a single parent, I knew I would need extra support. I suggested to my mother that we sell our condos and buy a house together. My mother could provide child care when I was working, and also have the opportunity to develop a close relationship with her granddaughter. We bought a large house with enough room for ourselves and for a friend to move in with us. She would provide extra income to make the house payment and be another adult in the house for child care. We all moved in with great anticipation. It was such a good plan.*

*However, nothing worked according to our idealized vision of "home." Combining three households of belongings did not make for an efficient or beautiful environment. We tried to merge three of everything, and had our biggest challenge in the kitchen. Where do you put three toasters, three mixers, three microwaves (four if you count the one that came with the house) and three sets of flatware? Combined we had so many dishes that we joked about having the capacity to feed several hundred people at the same time. With the kitchen counters and cabinets crammed full of triplicate items, we couldn't find anything when we needed to prepare a meal. And yet, no one volunteered to get rid of her belongings.*

*The other common areas in the house didn't fare much better. The living room and den were filled with furniture bought for other spaces, combining three very distinct tastes in décor and color schemes. The house was turned into a hodgepodge of this era and that, curlycue colonial next to sleek-line modern, Craftsman simplicity next to Asian micro-detail. What didn't fit into the house was stuffed downstairs in a basement. It was an interior decorator's nightmare.*

*We had hardly unpacked when, in 2004, I went to Nepal to complete the paperwork for the adoption of a little baby girl. I expected the process to take about two months; yet another good plan that didn't quite turn out as expected. I ended up spending nearly two years in Nepal before I brought Jenee, my daughter, home to the States.*

*While living in Nepal I saw poverty—real poverty—close up in a way I had never experienced it before. All of the water, even in the finest of hotels, was contaminated. The power was turned off anywhere from four to sixteen hours a day as Nepal experienced power shortages. I looked into the eyes of mothers living on the streets with their children while sick, stray dogs wandered, sniffing through trash for their next meal. They had next to nothing. And I had a house full of stuff. The discrepancy between my lifestyle and their struggle for survival hit me hard.*

*Once back in the U.S., my mother and I took a long, hard look at our lives and how we wanted to raise Jenee. I resented all of the objects that seemed to control my options. It was very expensive housing so much stuff. The upkeep on the house gobbled up money—a gardener for the front- and backyards, a pool service to keep our pool clean and functioning, and a house so large it required two water heaters, two furnaces, and two air conditioners. All of this added up to an electric bill that often topped $1,000 a month, not including water and gas.*

*Fire insurance, property taxes, house payments, and regular living*
*expenses resulted in a heavy financial burden. It was not good for any*
*of us, let alone my daughter, who picked up on my stress.*

*We decided it was time to downsize considerably. I sold the*
*house and we moved from over 4,000 square feet to 1,800. We sold*
*approximately 90 percent of our belongings. There were moments,*
*I'll admit, that I wasn't sure if I'd made good decisions about what to*
*keep and what to discard. But ultimately it was a relief to pull out of*

## Carmen's Definition of Clutter

For me, clutter differs from unfinished chores. The stack of unfolded laundry on my couch is very different from the pile of clothes on the floor of my closet. I know what to do about the unfolded laundry—fold it and put it away where it belongs. But there's no "place" for the pile of clothes on the floor of my closet. In fact, I'm not even sure what's in that pile. When I look at it, I feel overwhelmed and shut the closet door.

There's also a difference to me between clutter and storage. I store my Christmas decorations in clearly marked plastic bins. Every year, I know where to find them, and what is stored in them. Clutter, on the other hand, comprises the unmarked boxes in my garage that contain a conglomerate of things from old photos, paper clips, high school yearbooks, and junk. There's no rhyme or reason to what's in each box, and therefore no way to access the items when needed. Clutter triggers feelings of embarrassment and frustration, emotions that repel me rather than invite me toward it. I have a sense of accomplishment when I know how to access things when I need them. But the clutter? I just want to run in the opposite direction.

*the driveway with significantly fewer belongings and a fraction of the strain I had inflicted on myself.*

*We now live within our means—both financially and in terms of available space. And we're much happier. I'm investing myself in raising my daughter and in my new charity, Hope Partnership Nepal. I still have all of the memories I had before, without the excess baggage. It's much more satisfying to me to "travel light."*

# Let's Be Partners

We first met in 1997 through a mutual friend. After working on a few writing projects together, we lost contact with each other. Fast-forward to 2006 when Mark needed a writing consultant, and we got back in touch.

We got reacquainted over lunch. Carmen had been addressing stress management as a speaker and writer, and confronting the clutter in her life and the lives of her real estate clients. Mark was working in the trenches of clutter doing TV design, learning first-hand what worked and what didn't work with the participants on *Clean House*.

The topic of clutter came up and the difficulty we were both having with clearing out our homes. The more we shared our personal experiences, and drew from our combined expertise, the more insight and clarity was experienced. We agreed to meet again, and over the next few months, developed a new paradigm—one that had not been recognized in the home makeover industry to date. Through a series of insights and committed action, the way we viewed clutter was transformed, and we were thoroughly empowered to succeed! A true partnership was born. You are invited to join this partnership.

## Partner with Us

Much to our surprise, we became experts. Not experts on clutter, but experts on our own lives! This profound and eye-opening level of awareness allowed us to be genuinely authentic about the situation at hand and tackle the challenge of clutter in an entirely different way. With our new understanding, the obstacles to creating a clutter-free home diminished in relevance before our eyes. How we saw items in our homes, from the necessities to the needless stuff, looked altogether different. We both felt free of the frustration and filled with a sense of peace and underlying power. The ability to make decisions about things in our homes has become nearly effortless.

Looking back, this new way of seeing clutter seems so obvious to us, but for one reason or another, it wasn't until we joined forces that this paradigm revealed itself. If the truth will set you free, then this book will set you free from your clutter for it is grounded in the truth—the truth of who you are as a human being.

And now it's time for us to reveal it to you! We invite you to partner with us in this energizing journey—from clutter and discouragement to order and purpose. You are, of course, free to accept or decline our invitation. But we genuinely trust that by virtue of your reading this, you are interested in creating life-enhancing spaces that fit your life as we now enjoy in our lives.

As partners, we will all contribute equally in the process, bringing our individual creativity and passion forward. How can you partner with us in equal measure? By deciding to participate fully in the progression of steps we will lead you through. We encourage you to work through the exercises (not simply read them). They are deliberately created to empower and invigorate you, and at the same time bring you peace of mind. You are invited to engage with us to discover what you already know and to tap into the power you already possess—all of the riches that already reside in the Inner "U."

While you are reading this book and working through the process, we'd like you to make one promise: *Do not clear or organize anything in your home until it's time.* Don't fuss or fret over the mess in your family room, or the dust piling up on your collectibles in the hutch. Try not to even look around you, if that's what it takes to distance yourself from the clutter. Give yourself a "time-out" from feeling guilty or ashamed or helpless. Take a deep breath and go on this journey with us.

# Get the Most Out of This Process

We want to tell you up front that we had fun designing and working on the "Practices to Live Out, Follow, or Apply" so some of them might seem a bit ridiculous. Just because an exercise brings a smile to your face doesn't mean that it isn't a very important step toward your goal. Many of them remind us of the famous "wax on, wax off" scene in the movie, *The Karate Kid*. At first Daniel, played by Ralph Macchio, had no idea why his mentor, Mr. Miyagi, asked him to wash and wax so many cars. Only in the end did he realize that the movements in cleaning the cars were the same as those found in karate. For now, you may have no idea why you are doing a particular exercise. But we promise it will all come together and will make sense. We want you to have a good time freeing yourself from a cluttered home. Enough drudgery! Enough frustration! It's time to enjoy you!

This book is designed with spaces for you to write as you work through the practices. If you plan to pass this book on to someone else, which we hope you will, we recommend that you get a separate journal or notebook.

In addition to a place to write, you'll need a couple of other items to get the most out of the practices: one large poster board in any color, a pack of sticky notes, tape or glue, scissors, and a good pen or pencil. You may also need some magazines or newspapers from which to cut specific pictures. When working on these practices, we encourage you to turn off your TV and cell phone, and carve out uninterrupted time you will devote to this process. If you need another cup of tea, now is a good time for a refill.

We're in this together . . . Welcome to a new path of discovery!

## Practices to Live Out, Follow, or Apply

The first thing we want you to do is take a "before" picture of your clutter. Go room by room, area by area. Feel free to photograph the messiness from several angles. Get a really good visual of the extent—depth, height, every dimension—of the stuff you have stashed around your home.

Print out the pictures and study them. Take a good, long look at your surroundings. A cluttered space looks more pronounced in a picture than it might firsthand. Contemplate the word "clutter." Clutter is often defined as anything and everything that has accumulated in such a way that it hinders your livelihood, your relationships, your options for future growth and contribution. An article in Wikipedia defines clutter as "a confusing or disorderly state or collection; or the creation thereof." You may have your own definition of clutter. Please write out your definition in the space below or in your journal.

_____

_____

_____

After you've completed your definition, tape all of the pictures at the end of your journal, or on the back pages of this book. At the end of this process, we'll ask you to take pictures from the same vantage points. We're certain you'll be pleased by the changes that will have occurred within yourself and within your home.

## AFFIRMATIONS

At the end of each chapter will be affirmations that can serve as a focal point of meditation. We believe there is a lot of power in what we choose to focus on. Calm begats calm. Clarity begets clarity. Gratitude begets gratitude. On the other hand, asking ourselves "what is missing" will produce more that is missing. The affirmations we've written are meant to focus your attention on what brings empowerment into your life. Select an affirmation, close your eyes, and take several deep breaths. Repeat the affirmation in your mind as you meditate for several minutes, letting the truth take hold in your mind.

# 2

# You Are the Expert

Regina is a retired registered nurse who cooks every day and delivers food baskets to people in her neighborhood who are facing difficulties. She provides meals for working single parents, elderly friends who have trouble getting to the store, and people who have been laid off from their jobs. To others, she is a source of encouragement. Those who depend on her generosity would have no reason to know that Regina lives in a home full of clutter that burdens her with an emotional cloud of helplessness.

Regina told us:

*I called Mark for help. I led him to the kitchen where I was cooking up some dinners. Despite the enticing aroma of an array of comfort food that had just come out of the oven, Mark seemed a bit stunned by the sight of boxes of flour, rice, and other ingredients and kitchen appliances stacked up on every surface in my kitchen. On top of all the mess sat a number of home organizing books and magazines. Before he could say anything, I told him, "I seem to have no problem making sure that everyone on my food list gets hot meals. And yet I can't seem to get a handle on this mess. I've bought everything I can find on the market to get started, but I never quite get things under control. I don't have time to get organized! I'm too busy cooking and helping people."*

*Mark asked me how I was able to pack the many meals I delivered without at least one clean area in which to work. I confessed, "When it comes to the clutter, I feel completely overwhelmed and helpless. I just work on top of the junk. That's why I've contacted you, Mark. I need help."*

*As Mark walked across the kitchen floor, there was crackling under his feet. He noticed 12x12 stone tiles that had been set in place but were never grouted, leaving half-inch gaps between each tile. The gaps were filled with food crumbs and accumulated dirt. I watched him notice a thin layer of grease that had built up on the kitchen cabinetry. In the far corner, a commercial-grade deep fryer was full of cooking grease, yet there was no proper hood for ventilation. The entire kitchen was a grease fire waiting to happen. How did I lose control over my own home?*

## How Did You Lose Your Self-Confidence?

Asking for help when you need it is nothing to be ashamed of. Everyone needs help at various times in life. But we want to pause and ask you to think about something for a moment. Regina is a competent, reliable woman who cares for other people who depend on her. And yet, she feels unable to care for her own space. Where did she get the idea that she can properly respond to the needs of others but can't adequately address her own needs for a clean, orderly working area? While feeling competent enough to rely on her own judgment regarding other areas of her life, what undermines her confidence so that she feels the need to call in an "expert" to deal with her home organization challenge?

We believe Regina's lack of self-confidence is founded, at least in part, in the unspoken message of powerlessness given by the clutter industry. By relying on experts, rather than on her own sense of self, her sense of personal power was undermined. Gaining ideas from someone else who has traveled the same road can be genuinely helpful. But *deferring* to someone else's direction is, by definition, a loss of personal power. Like Regina, you may have unwittingly been influenced by the message: *Your house is a mess, therefore you are a mess. Since you are a mess, you can't trust yourself to clean up the mess. Rely on us, the experts.*

Regina was well aware that her house, especially her kitchen, was chaotic. But rather than tap into her sense of competence, Regina was led to believe that she couldn't be successful in organizing her home. She was told that she needed an expert to tell her what to do. Perhaps you've felt this, too.

■ ■ ■

*The clutter industry is growing because it doesn't help people simplify their living spaces.*

■ ■ ■

The clutter industry is not growing because it genuinely helps people; rather *the clutter industry is growing because it doesn't help people simplify their living spaces.* While the self-help industry may intend to empower people, it is also a disempowering force, keeping people from achieving their potential. Books are written by "experts" in their field, and we, as readers, are expected to follow the advice of the experts. But when we look to someone else to have the answers for our lives, we give our power away and we become powerless.

Take a look around you. In spite of the massive information available to us, our homes are still filled with gifts we can no longer use (or never liked in the first place), computers that no longer work, magazines filled with irrelevant articles, and a variety of objects that we can't seem to let go of. Many of us are hoarding just plain junk that nobody else would carry off if it were free for the taking. Even in times of economic hardship Americans continually accumulate more clutter, not less. In fact, financial insecurity may even exacerbate one's fear of scarcity, resulting in an increased need to cling to belongings. Perhaps the worst consequence is, along with the clutter you already have, you may also be adding stacks of organizing books, plastic bins, and piles of shelving that never get set up or used! As consumers, we put our faith in the experts to tell us what to do and then we don't do it.

*Clutter Confessions*

## Carmen

It has been easy for me to have a burst of energy when trying a new organizing strategy. More than once I've gotten color-coordinated file folders, new dividers, and color sticky dots and attacked a large stack of unsorted paper piling up around my desk. It's fun at first, but pretty rapidly I lose steam. Before long, I can't remember where I filed certain papers and it's discouraging. I've often thought to myself, "It's better to keep my papers on the floor. At least that way I know it's all here in this stack someplace!"

## You Are the Expert

We would like to invite you to try something. And as you do, think of this exercise as if you are trying on a hat at your favorite store. You put it on, look at yourself in the mirror, and see how well it suits you. You have the chance to consider the price and style, and ultimately choose whether the look and feel it gives is something you want. If it doesn't fit, you don't have to buy it.

In the same way, we'd like you to try on the possibility that YOU are the expert on your life. We believe that one of the biggest gaps between the so-called experts and you is this: Only *you* know who you really are, how you want to live and what's ultimately most important at this stage of your life. You know what you like to eat and what tastes make you grimace. Only you know what energizes you, what your secret dreams are, and what you'd most love to do with your life. Only you are the real expert on YOU and know what is truly important to you. You know what kind of people you enjoy and those you try to avoid. You, and only you, are the expert on who you are and what you want.

You are the expert. You, and only you.

You might be saying to yourself, "I'm the expert? Yeah, right. I'm an expert in leaving my clothes all over my bedroom. I'm an expert in collecting so many pieces of pottery that my family no longer has space to eat at the table. I'm the one to ask if your goal is to stack paper, files, and other supplies all over my

■ ■ ■

*You, and only you, are the expert on who you are and what you want.*

■ ■ ■

home office so that there's no floor space, only a narrow path to the desk."

So you ARE an expert—you're an expert at leaving your clothes all over the bedroom, collecting pottery, stacking paper and other office supplies, and generally cluttering up your home. Let's start with this admission: You are an expert on collecting clutter in your own unique style. It's simply time to channel that expertise in a new direction and let it grow and flourish.

Who's really in charge here? Are you the keeper of clutter or is the clutter the keeper of you? Until you accept that you are the keeper of yourself in all matters, it will be natural for you to rely on someone else to fill the position. In the case of your home, it's often organizational experts. But truth be told, they are just filling in during your temporary absence. They have strategically filled this spot in your life where you have yet to fully step in. And although it's sometimes easier to let someone else tell you what to do, most often, the results are not what you really want. We are willing to bet that as things accumulated in your home, you felt overwhelmed and looked for someone else to tell you what to do. You may not have realized that your need for an expert was based on your limiting belief that you genuinely needed someone else to tell you what to do. It's time to step into the gap. It's time to step into your power.

"But wait a minute," you might say to yourself. "Mark and Carmen are telling me I'm the expert in a self-help book. Why are they writing this book if they aren't experts?"

We believe that a self-help book that can genuinely assist you in your journey is one that fosters a deeper understanding of who you are, empowering *you* to choose what works best for you. We've found that knowledge isn't always power and insight isn't enough to enable us to make sustainable change. The most useful information is that which creates the space for people to make decisions for themselves. This is a process that allows people to get to know themselves on a deeper level and supports them in making choices that emanate from who they really are—not from someone else's point of view, but their own.

This book, while in the self-help category, is written from the vantage point that we do not know what is best for your life. You will discover your own way through experimentation and exploration, but not merely by reading. Rather than being full of facts and techniques that your brain can absorb, we have designed this book to be experiential. We offer strategies, a series of actions that reinforce your confidence rather than burden you with another to-do list. Despite the belief that information is power, we discovered that what's missing is the *motivation* to work through this process to completion, which is why we ask you to take your time moving through each section. We encourage you to do the practices, not simply read through them and pretend to do them. They were designed to have a layering effect.

We will guide you to deeper discovery, but only you can create the approach to home organization that will work effectively for you. Sure, we will be there to guide you, but in order for us to assist you, we need to deal directly with the person in charge. The person in charge of your life. YOU. Together, we can affirm your ability to succeed in your desire to have an orderly, beautiful home. We want you to know that we believe in you and, in fact, we wouldn't have it any other way.

## What Powerlessness Looks Like

Okay, so let's assume that you're pondering the idea that you are the expert on your life and that we won't instruct you on what kind of organizational system you should use. To help you better understand what is at stake, we ask you to walk into a room or an area that frustrates you the most. We mean it. Please pick up the book and walk to that area.

Once you're there, look around. THIS, my friend, is what thinking you need so-called experts has produced in your life. THIS is what not relying on yourself to be the expert on your life looks like. THIS triggers the feelings you are experiencing when looking at the mess in front of you. *This* is what it looks and feels like to give your power away.

We've all heard the expression *riding shotgun.* In this case, every time you believe that you are not the expert on you, you are handing over the wheel. Although you may still be in the front seat and it may appear that you are driving, you are simply a passenger in your own life allowing someone or something else to steer. The results are right in front of you. All of the actions you HAVE been taking and whatever you HAVEN'T been doing up to this point are what got you here.

The result? Your life is harder, not easier. You experience less confidence and an outcome that is unsatisfactory. You end up in a place you never intended to go. We believe with 100 percent certainty that the moment you embrace the fact that you are the true expert on your life, you gain your power back. You move from the passenger seat to the driver's seat. This doesn't mean that you will suddenly have all the answers. It simply means that you are willing to answer for yourself. And when you do, your hands are on the wheel and your power instantly returns. When you are in the driver's seat, you experience an innate sense of play, ease, and exhilaration and life becomes more and more effortless. It's your own *power* steering!

It's time to walk in the truth, not the scripted advice by so-called experts. It's time to create a roadmap for decluttering your home based on your life experiences and deep-rooted passions, no longer being swayed by short-lived fads or shallow commercialism. It's time to take an honest look at your clutter, and thereby come to a deeper understanding of yourself and get on with your life.

The key difference between engaging in a partnership with us and deferring your power to another expert is revealed in the level of accountability. In a partnership, everyone involved is held 100 percent accountable. When you defer your power, the responsibility is divided. Someone has to take the blame for the inevitable failure.

We respect and acknowledge that you are in complete control of your life, the one making decisions. Some of the outcomes of your decisions may not be exactly what you intended. That's fine. We expect you to experiment with strategies and proposed actions. This is a learning process, not a single event or action. As you engage in the process, you'll discover more about yourself and your decision-making process. By honing your decision-making skills versus your "organizing" skills, you will be more equipped to deal with clutter in the long-term.

You have control over the choices you make. As your partners, we demonstrate our respect for you by holding you, and only you, accountable. As you acknowledge that you are the expert on your life, you make all the decisions that will lead to a clutter-free home. Ironically, until you declare yourself the expert on your life, we will not be able to assist you fully. Our expertise can only be accessed by people who take responsibility for their choices.

We can ride shotgun only if someone else is driving. You are the only one who can be at the wheel.

> *By honing your decision-making skills versus your "organizing" skills, you will be more equipped to deal with clutter in the long-term.*

The change in seating position alone will begin to offer a fresh, new perspective.

## Discard the Blame Game

It may sound contradictory: We are holding you responsible for giving your power away. But that is where we need to start. The bottom line is that you, directly or indirectly, are responsible for the clutter in your house.

When you hear that we are holding you responsible for all the decisions that led to your current living situation, you may feel we are blaming you. You may think, "That's not true. My spouse [children, roommate, parents, etc.] live here, too, and most of this stuff is theirs!" You may want to blame someone else or begin running a litany of excuses as to why your house looks the way it does. If you are thinking that now, you are in the perfect place. Thank you for being honest.

Let's keep this honesty going. We would like for you to make a list and write down every possible reason or excuse that your place looks the way it does. You might write, "I don't have time to clean up" or "Organization is not my thing" or on the contrary, "I'm an organized person, it's my husband that is the slob." Or, "I don't have a place to put anything" or "My place is too small and I have too much stuff." Whatever comes to mind, write it down.

We know that many people can come into play in a household so we don't want you to feel as though we are ganging up on you. There are many layers to decision-making and many factors influence the clutter created in your home. The people who live with you are extremely important and may also need to be challenged to reclaim their power and space. We will address these issues in more depth later in the book. But regardless of how many people are involved in the decision, you play a significant part in creating a cluttered environment. Until you own your role, you won't be able to access your personal power. The power to claim your clutter and reclaim your life. The result is permanent life change.

Review the list you created and notice how you contributed to the clutter by the actions you've taken, or your inactivity. You have, at the very least, allowed these conditions to exist. You may be like us. At one point or another we have said, "I just cannot deal with all of this mess!" But then we came to realize that we *were* dealing with it—by refusing to deal with it. The plan of action was avoidance.

You chose the schedule that prevents you from cleaning up, you chose to marry the man you say is a slob and you chose the place in which you live, which has limited storage space. You chose it all. You may not have placed that particular shirt on the floor or that magazine on the table. But by virtue of letting the shirt remain on the floor or the magazine stay on the table, you have made a choice. By taking no action, you clearly communicate the clutter is acceptable—at least for now.

You may be saying to yourself, "This situation is unacceptable!" We hope you're saying that. Because when you are honest about your situation, you are honest with yourself. This is the starting point for accessing your true power. As we walk through this process, we want to empower you, not blame you or anyone else. It is only when you take care of yourself that you will be able to take care of others in such a way that doesn't compromise who you are. We invite you to be the expert on your life and take full responsibility for your home. It's time to stand in your power and walk with us in the truth. Open yourself to the possibility that, by the end of this process, you will be proficient in organizing your home and creating the living environment of your dreams.

## Practices to Live Out, Follow, or Apply

We have just introduced to you a new concept, a new distinction, called "I am the expert on my life." By the time we finish you're going to be amazed at what you already know about yourself, what's best for you, and how to go about achieving it.

Wonderful Things About Me:

Below or in your journal, list at least ten traits or skills you have that you admire; ten things that work about you. Don't worry if these things have nothing to do with cleaning your house. List things such as "I take good care of my friends," "I am trustworthy," "I am good with my finances," "I work hard at my career," "I know how to make gorgeous flower arrangements," or "I am good in the kitchen."

1. _____

2. _____

3. _____

4. _____

5. _____

6. _____

7. _____

8. _____

9. _____

10. _____

- Read over this list and note how your body feels when you reflect upon things you like about yourself. Do you sit up taller? Do you breathe more deeply? Does a slight smile come to your face? Do you feel more energetic? Write these down in your journal.

- Notice that when you focus on the things you do well, you gain energy and optimism. The calming endorphins begin to flow. Endorphins are neurotransmitters produced in the brain that reduce pain and have been known to induce euphoria. It's an instant, feel-good moment you experience after you exercise, laugh at something, or simply have a positive perspective on life.

## Tag Your Clutter:

Place a sticky note on ten items in your home that by your definition you consider clutter. These items might be expensive antiques or dollar-store purchases, things you've had many years or items you've recently acquired. You can pick ten items in one room or identify clutter all over the house. Leave the sticky notes on these items. We'll be using them in later chapters.

## AFFIRMATIONS

- I intuitively know that I am always on track.

- I am trusting in the freedom of knowing what's best for me in my home and in my heart.

- When it comes to my life, I am in the driver's seat. There is no harm in that.

- I have faith that, once I have completed this process, I will have an organized home that will fill me with positive and empowering emotions.

- I know what energizes me, my secret dreams, and what I'd most love to do with my life. I am my own expert.

- I keep my clutter, it doesn't keep me. I am the keeper of my life.

# 3

# Your House May Be a Mess, But You Are Not

Lila, a freelance photographer, was very reluctant to invite Mark over to her home. Lila remembers:

*I was so torn about letting Mark actually see what my house was like. I needed his help, but I didn't want him to come into the house. It may sound crazy, but I was really scared about it. Mark is a very intuitive person, and I was afraid he'd look around and be able to see into the depth of my soul.*

*When he came into my entry I sighed. "I'm such a mess. I really need help."*

*Mark looked around at the clutter strewn all over the floor of the hallway and intersecting rooms. He smiled at me and said, "I can see that your house is messy, Lila. But that doesn't mean that you are a mess. It just means that your house is a mess."*

*I'd never thought if it that way before. Until that moment, I guess I had equated myself with my house! If it was a mess, than I assumed I was a mess, too.*

## Your House Is a Mess

Both of us have felt nervous, from time to time, inviting people to our homes. Haven't you? When we invite people into our homes, we welcome them into the space we have created for ourselves—a space that can speak volumes about how we perceive and care for ourselves. When friends or family come over, we imagine what our homes look like through their eyes. It's easy to assume that their reaction has at least a hint of criticism. This is especially true if our homes are full of clutter.

Here are some of the things that might go through our minds:

"What do my friends think of me with all that junk in the dining room?"

"I wonder if my aunt noticed that I have all of the figurines she has given me in the living room. Well, it is a little hard to see them behind the stack of magazines I tossed on the shelf."

"I'll try to keep everyone in the family room. I hope no one goes into any of the bedrooms. I've shut all of the bedroom doors since they're all a mess."

## You Are Not Your House

You are not your house. It may seem like this doesn't need to be stated, but we have found that many people confuse their identities and self-esteem with the quality and cleanliness of their homes.

It's easier than you might think at first glance to get yourself confused with the structure in which you live. You may so deeply identify yourself, and your sense of self-worth, with your home that you no longer differentiate yourself from your house.

But, you may be thinking, "I am the one who is responsible for the mess in my house. Of course my home reflects on me." Let's take a look at the difference between responsibility and a sense of self-worth. They are, in fact, two very different things. While it's true that you have the power to make changes in your life, your life is of infinite value no matter what you do or don't do. Lila had the same problem.

*Mark asked me to look into the mirror hanging on my entry wall. So I did. Mark asked, "What do you see, Lila? Do you see a man-made structure with a roof and walls and plumbing? Do you see a fireplace or a kitchen sink? Do you have spaces inside of you big enough to hold a sofa or a dining room table?"*

*I laughed. "No, of course not. I see me."*

*"That's right, Lila," Mark continued. "You see a human being, not a building. You are a person, and your house is . . . well . . . a house."*

We'd like you to do a quick exercise to help make our point. Go to the next page or go to a blank page in your journal and draw a line down the center. Now draw a picture of your house on the left side of a page and

a picture of yourself on the right. Have fun with this exercise and be as artsy as you'd like. But don't get bogged down on the picture itself. You don't need to be an artist. It's fine to draw yourself and your house like a little child might.

Once you've completed the drawing, write your name underneath the drawing you made of yourself. Under the house you drew, write out the address of that home. Please notice that you and the house are two separate entities.

Consider this: There was a time when you did not live in this house and there will be a time when you will leave this house. But no matter where you live, you will still be you and the house will still be the house. In fact, if your house and everything in it was washed away in a flood tomorrow, you would still be you.

## The Worth of Your Home Does Not Determine Your Worth As a Human Being

We live in a global society that overly values the accumulation of wealth. It's easy to fall prey to the idea that our personal value is determined by our financial status. Have you ever heard the phrase, "I wonder how much he's worth?" This question is meant to address the amount of wealth a person has accumulated. But that's not what the words actually say. It implies that people who are wealthy are "worth" more than people of lesser means. Our distorted values reveal when we equate "finances" with "worth." Some people may believe they are more important than others because they live in large homes filled with the most expensive furniture they can find. But this is not true. Our worth is not determined by the value of our homes.

* * *

Lila recalls:

*I had to laugh when Mark pointed this out to me. When I first bought my home in the 1970s, it was worth around $30,000. A couple of years ago my home appraised for nearly ten times that much. Then recently the bottom dropped out of the real estate market and I'm sure this place is worth much less now. It's foolish to think that I was once ten times more valuable than I was in the seventies. Or that I'm any less significant now that the value of my home has plummeted.*

Lila has a good point. She is one of many who have recently been challenged to separate their sense of value from the appraisal of their homes. During the economic difficulties many are experiencing, it's vitally important that we don't base our self-esteem and sense of self-worth on something as unpredictable and ever-changing as home ownership or financial holdings. Now is a time of placing one's self-worth on

*Clutter Confessions*

## Mark

I used to feel the need to impress people with my décor instead of placing a genuine emphasis on me. I figured if I could wow people with my furnishings, it would distract them from my shortcomings. Now that I've taken the time to write down what really matters to me, my purpose and passion have taken center stage. They are the focal points in my life.

a solid spiritual foundation that includes love, talents, service to others, and other significant parts of your life that do not drop or rise with the stock market.

Look back at your drawing. Underneath the house drawing, write a numerical estimate of what your home might appraise for in today's market. Now, underneath your picture, estimate your personal worth. You might want to write "infinite value" or "priceless." You are alive with potential and possibilities and dreams. You can't put a price tag on who you are now and who you are becoming but you can put a price tag on your home.

We believe that every human being has worth and significance regardless of how many possessions accumulated. We are individuals of worth, and are all born with innate value, skills, and talents. We do not become more valuable because we live in a home with larger square footage. Nor do we decrease in self-worth when the estimated value of our homes and holdings diminishes.

## You Are Not Your Clutter

In the same way that you are not your house, it's critical that you not equate yourself with your clutter. You are not a pile of clothes draped across your bed, a garage packed full with keepsakes, or a collection of vases crammed into your front hall. You aren't a mountain of boxes full of disheveled sewing supplies and antique lace. Nor are you the mismatched tools rusting out back in the shed. You are a human being and your clutter is stuff. Please don't mistake the two as one and the same.

Accepting this has been difficult for both of us. It may be hard for you, too. Distinguishing your "self" from your belongings is at the heart of our process. It's taking the "U" out of clutter.

Mark's client Lila certainly struggled when he told her that the clutter in her house didn't define her any more than her home appraisal.

Lila said:

*I told Mark, "You're not convincing me that the mess in this house isn't my fault. If I were a better person, more disciplined or more some-thing, my house would be neat and clean."*

*Mark said, "When we're finished working together, your home will be clutter-free. Do you believe that?"*

*I told him, "I hope that's true."*

*"So, when your home is clean, will you be a better person than you are now?"*

*I thought about this for a moment. "No, I'll be just the same as I am now, only no longer living with all this junk around me."*

*Mark nodded. "That's right. You'll still be you. Only you'll live in a cleaner house. We are going to solve your clutter problem. You can count on that. But YOU are not the problem."*

At some time in your life, you have accomplished a goal you had set for yourself. How did you feel after you succeeded? Most of us feel really good about ourselves when we master a skill, complete a project, or win a contest. After all the effort we put into our goals, we gift ourselves with a feeling of self-esteem. We feel good about ourselves, not because we are "better" or more valuable than we were before, but because we felt that we had *earned the right* to experience that feeling.

Let's try an experiment. Look over at some of the clutter you have around you. In your journal, write and say out loud, "My house is a mess because I am a mess." Concentrate on the phrase, let this idea sink in. Notice what your body is doing. Are you holding your breath? Are you clinching your jaw? Are your neck muscles tensing up? How does this make you feel about yourself? Energized and ready to take on new challenges, optimistic? Or discouraged and distracted?

ON THE FOLLOWING PAGE OR IN YOUR JOURNAL, WRITE THIS PHRASE OVER AND OVER:

"My house is a mess because I am a mess."

"My house is a mess because I am a mess."

"My house is a mess because I am a mess."

"My house is a mess because I am a mess."

"My house is a mess because I am a mess."

"My house is a mess because I am a mess."

Let each word take effect. Write it until the phrase seems as absurd to you as it really is. You may need to write it ten times, fifty times, or one hundred times. Write it until you can't stand to write it anymore. Do you *really* believe what you are writing? Do you really believe that your worth as a human being is determined by the value of your house or better yet, the clutter inside of your house? Don't stop until you start

My house is a mess because I am a mess.

_____

_____

_____

_____

_____

_____

_____

_____

_____

to smile. When you are sick and tired of writing it, see if you can write it ten more times.

The truth is your house may be a mess, but you are not. Be careful not to collapse the two into one—you and the house are two distinct entities. You aren't broken or defective or in some way unworthy. A messy house is simply a messy house. You are you. You are not your clutter.

Now, on the next blank page or on a new page in your journal, draw yourself on the right side. This time, on the left side draw your clutter. Don't get hung up on detailing it. Just draw a bunch of squiggles that represent what you've got stashed around the house. Now draw a thick line between you and the clutter.

Write "My house is a mess and I am me!" Write it a number of times, letting the truth sink in. Once again, notice how your body is reacting. Did you take a deep breath or let out a sigh? Is there a slight smile on your face? Are your neck muscles relaxing a bit? Imagine feeling good about yourself right now, not waiting until some time off in the distant future. Continue to write this phrase until you see the truth in it and really believe it. Your body will confirm that you are heading in a positive direction. Follow the path that brings you more health and happiness. Make a distinction between you and your clutter, not because it feels good, but because it is true. You are not your clutter.

Why is making this distinction so important? Because as long as you define yourself by your stuff, you're going to stay stuck. You put yourself under stress that is not based in reality, the kind of stress that doesn't motivate people to effective action. It might cause our bodies to pump adrenaline into our bloodstream, but that extra energy won't produce lasting change. It will just make you feel badly about yourself. Poor self-esteem is a lousy motivator for positive action.

A lot of us try to motivate ourselves to do good things by feeling badly about ourselves. If that approach worked, we might support it. But it doesn't. At every moment, we have the opportunity to experience a positive and true sense of self. We encourage you to stop depriving yourself of feeling good about yourself. Stop waiting to feel good about who you are until you feel you've earned it. When you think about it for a moment, it's obvious why that approach doesn't work. Withholding positive regard does not make us want to work harder. It makes us feel tired and overwhelmed and helpless. We have less energy, not more. It doesn't work, and that is no way to live your life.

You don't need a clean house to feel good about yourself. You can feel good about yourself right now. Immediately. There's no reason to wait. You may want to start by saying one of the wonderful things you wrote down about yourself in the last chapter. Self-esteem is a choice. It's a gift you give yourself. Rearranging all of your belongings will not make you a better person. You can give yourself permission to have good self-esteem and still have clutter in your house because . . . why? You are not your clutter!

Nor are you defined by your challenges. Everyone in this world has difficulties. No one is immune to loss, disappointment, and unwanted change. None of us are defined by the challenges we face. We develop and illustrate our true self, however, by how we handle life's challenges.

One of the challenges in your life is clutter. By following the steps we have outlined here, you will have the opportunity to see clutter not as a source of shame or guilt but as an opportunity for personal growth and development. Turn your irritation on its head and say, "I am so grateful for this clutter!" You don't merely have a pile of unsorted family photos, a stack of knitting magazines, or a playroom that is so stuffed with toys that there is no place to play—you have windows of opportunity to the life you've always wanted to lead. In fact, clutter can show you the way if you let it.

Make a decision right now to see clutter not as a stumbling block but as an opportunity to make an informed decision about what's important to you and those things that you truly desire in your home. The cool part? Once you go through the decision-making process a couple of times, it will soon become old hat. Like a recipe that you have to follow carefully the first few times, before you know it, you are able to make the dish by memory. It becomes automatic.

## Practices to Live Out, Follow, or Apply

It might be tempting to skip this exercise because it's so simple it might seem rather silly. But it's important that you let the message of this chapter sink in.

1. Go to the items upon which you placed the ten sticky notes, as specified in the last chapter.

2. Write on each note the price you could sell this item for in today's market.

3. Below or in your journal list each item and the monetary value, and add for a total value.

4. Ask yourself the question, "Do I believe I am worth more than the total monetary value of these ten items?" Another question to ask is, "If I put a monetary value on everything in my home, would

I be worth more than the total of my belongings?" The answer to both, of course, is a resounding YES! You are of infinite value. Take some time to think about the dangers of equating your self-worth with what you own.

$ _____   $ _____

$ _____   $ _____

$ _____   $ _____

$ _____   $ _____

$ _____   $ _____

Total $ _____

## AFFIRMATIONS

- I am not my home.

- I am worthy regardless of the value or condition of my home.

- I am not my clutter.

- I feel good about myself right now.

- Addressing the clutter in my house is an opportunity for personal growth.

# 4

# Everything in Your Home Has a Story

Twenty-nine-year-old Marguerite invited Mark over to the apartment she and her new husband shared. She recalled:

*We stood at the door of the dining room that was stuffed with boxes of wedding gifts, most of which were unopened. Even though my husband, Bruce, and I had been married for nearly six months, we still hadn't settled in.*

*I told Mark, "I am so embarrassed that I haven't unwrapped all of these presents yet. I can't invite anyone over in case they'll find out their gift is still sitting in the dining room. I don't know what to do with all this junk."*

*Mark said, "There isn't any junk in this room."*

"What?" I said. "I thought you were going to help me get rid of all this clutter."

"I am." Mark told me. "But I'm not going to shame you, or call your belongings negative names. Every item in this room has an important story attached to it. This is a room full of stories, not junk."

Mark picked up a blender, still in the box. "Tell me the story about this item."

Without hesitation, I told him, "That is a gift from my father's new wife. If I ever had that in my kitchen my mother would be so upset."

He pointed to another blender. "And that one?"

"To tell you the truth," I said, "I don't know who gave me that. The cards were mixed up when the gifts were brought here from the reception. I can't get myself to admit to my friends that I don't know who gave me some of these things."

Mark smiled. "See? You have a story for every item in your dining room, in your entire house, actually. Even if that story is 'I wonder who gave me this?'"

A light went on inside my head. I could see what Mark was saying—I didn't simply have a room full of clutter. I had a room full of stories!

Mark continued, "Not only do you have a room full of stories, you have a room full of stories that mean something to you. Each item evokes an emotion, maybe even more than one feeling. When your feelings get overwhelming, it's extremely hard to clean the outward clutter. I'd like to take you through a process of addressing the inner emotions and stories before we do anything in your dining room."

I let out a big sigh, as if I'd been holding my breath for a long time. "I'd like that, Mark."

## Everything Has a Story

Everything has a story. Yes, it's true. There is a story attached to every item in your possession—from the extra paper clips to the sterling candle holders, from the pile of blankets and quilts to the disorganized jewelry-making supplies.

Have you noticed that it's much easier cleaning up a friend's clutter than your own? It's not hard to look over someone else's stuff and decide what to keep and what to toss. After all, the stuff is . . . well, it's just stuff. Broken toys are simply broken toys. Bolts of unused cloth are nothing more than bolts of unused cloth. Ten years of *National Geographic* magazines are outdated magazines that are taking up space. It is easy to sort through other people's belongings because you are not attached to them. You do not have a story about them.

But your friend knows the stories connected to her belongings. She looks at the same broken toys and remembers the hours of fun she had with them when she was a little girl. The same bolts of unused cloth are sewing projects she hopes to complete someday. She may treasure the *National Geographic* magazines because her father collected them.

The same thing happens to you when trying to sort through your belongings. You look at the mountain of Christmas wrap you collected since your child's first holiday and start recalling that special holiday when she got her first bike, or a new guitar. The next thing you know, you feel nostalgic and have the urge to go inside and call your daughter to see how she and your grandkids are doing.

What about that croquet set that's taking up room in your den? The mallets are dented and most of the balls are missing. But they remind you of vacations spent with your family at the lake house. When you pick up a mallet, it seems like you can still smell the freshly cut grass on the lawn where you and your brothers played together. No, it's just too hard to sell them at the yard sale.

Or maybe you open up a box of chipped dishes you've carried around with you since college. Your first boyfriend gave you a set of inexpensive tableware, and even though they're chipped and you're happily married to someone else, it feels like giving up young love if you let them go. We've all experienced a time when we were mired down in "remembering when."

*Clutter* Confessions

## Carmen

When I was in high school, my uncle painted a mountain scene in oils that I thought was pretty good at the time. He gave it to me for Christmas and I was thrilled. I lived in a cabin in the mountains north of Los Angeles and it fit perfectly in the living room. After ten years or so I sold the cabin and moved all of the furnishings into my new condo. My tastes had changed considerably and I decorated the living room in a more contemporary style using grays and burgundy accessories. Without thinking, I put my uncle's painting on the wall. A friend came over and commented that the painting looked odd amidst the current décor. When I looked at the room from her perspective I realized that the painting didn't fit at all. Plus I couldn't imagine decorating in a mountain motif again. I felt somewhat obligated to keep it since it was a gift, but I if I was honest, I would never buy a painting like it. So I took it down and donated it to a local thrift store. I'm sure someone else is enjoying it right now.

You Make the Meaning

## Every Story Is Important

Stories are important; whether they are long or short, complicated or simple. Why? Because they come together to tell the story of your life—your childhood, your romances, your children, your accomplishments, your hopes and dreams. They describe where you've been, point to where you might be stuck, and determine your options in the future.

The stories we tell about our belongings can have a powerful hold on us. In fact, the hold they have on us is as strong as our attachment to our loved ones and our past. These are very strong connections. Your stories help define who you are and who you love.

Let's look at this from a different angle. Imagine what it would be like if none of your belongings had stories. It would feel like sitting in someone else's house, someone you had never met or knew anything about. Even if you liked the décor, you wouldn't feel at home. These items would be "storyless" since they did not conjure up any associations or stories. You might actually have this experience if you sat down in a furniture store, surrounded by beautiful things, but nothing that belonged to you.

*Your stories turn a house full of stuff into your home full of memories.* If the vase that you got on your honeymoon was stripped of your attachment to the memory of your honeymoon, what would the vase become? The vase would simply be "a vase." That's all. Just a vase.

Your grandfather's decoy duck collection that he gave you right before he passed away would simply become "the decoy duck collection" that has been collecting dust in the attic for twenty years. The painting your cousin gave you—you know the one that doesn't match your taste or color scheme—would simply become "a painting" that hangs above your fireplace.

∗ ∗ ∗

Without an attachment to the people you love and the memories you cherish, your stuff would simply be "stuff." Distinguishing your attachment *to* your belongings *from* your belongings themselves is the next critical step in this process of self-empowerment. Your stories are invisible. Your clutter is not. Your heart can never be too full, but your house can.

When you redefine clutter from this perspective, it's easy to see that the items themselves are not at the heart of the problem. Rather, you have trouble clearing out the clutter because of your attachment to the memories these objects inspire. Your stories keep you stuck, not the item itself.

*Your heart can never be too full, but your house can.*

At this point, you might be thinking that we are stating the obvious. *Of course* the problem with dealing with clutter is our attachment to things. But it isn't obvious, not in a life-changing way, to most of us. We may know this in our minds, but not in a way that gives us access to our power and energizes us to action. We continue to keep the items that remind us of stories we want to remember or stories we've yet to resolve. It's time to change the focus from the clutter itself to those stories, your stories.

Placing your awareness on your stories might seem like bad news. But it isn't. We are offering you a revolutionary way of viewing the possibilities around you and your stuff, and ultimately, your life. We have traveled this path and we know how difficult and overwhelming this process can seem at times. But keep moving forward in this book, and in your journey. These new distinctions will become the tools of building the life you genuinely desire—a future worthy of who you were created to be.

## Practices to Live Out, Follow, or Apply

For the next few minutes, think about the chair you're sitting on right now. To an onlooker, the chair may simply be a chair, but not to you, because it's *your* chair. Since it is your chair it has a story. It may be a simple story such as "I bought this chair at a yard sale and I find it very comfortable." Or maybe it's a story about a tense relationship such as "This chair was given to me by my mother-in-law and I've never liked it but she'd get her feelings hurt if I got rid of it." Maybe it's a long, complicated tale like the story of Mark's grandmother and the organ she played for him as a child. Or a story of the shortwave radio Carmen and her dad built years ago.

What is the story of your chair? In the space below or in your journal, tell the story of your chair. Start with describing how this chair came into your possession. Did you pick it up last week or twenty years ago? Have you had it since your godmother passed away? Or something you kept after the divorce? Write out the memories it triggers in your mind.

_____

_____

_____

You've just told the story of how the chair came into your possession. Next tell the story of how this particular chair ended up in this particular room. Did you put the chair here because it enhances the beauty of the room, or does it clash with the color scheme? Have you begrudgingly dragged it from home to home? Was it selected for this specific place? Is it a reminder of your family heritage and serves as a source of pride, or something you feel guilty throwing out?

■ ■ ■

*You're attached to the story that you've attached to your belongings.*

■ ■ ■

You may have thought you are sitting on a chair, but in fact you are sitting on a story. It's your chair. It's your story. It's a story that only you can tell. No one else in your family can tell the story you tell about this chair because you each have your own story to tell about the chair. But you are the expert on this chair because the story you tell about it is yours and yours alone.

Pick out another item in your home—and you'll find there's a story attached to it. You're attached to the story that you've attached to your belongings. It's that simple, and why it's so hard to clear out the mess. The truth is we're not attached to the Christmas wrap, the chipped dishes, or the croquet set, per se. We're attached to the story that these items remind us to recall. Once you start reliving stories of your past, enjoyable or not, the next thing you know you've lost all motivation for organizing the room.

- Go to each sticky note you placed on items around your house. Before you take the sticky note away with you, write one or two words that describe the object.

- After you have gathered up all of the sticky notes, sit down and rate your attachment to the object from 1 to 10, with 1 being the least and 10 being the highest degree of attachment. Write the number on the sticky note.

- Observe how your body reacts when you think about these items. Do you find yourself holding your breath? Are you chewing your lip or nervously tapping your foot? Are your shoulders slumped as if weighed down?

- Resist any temptation to do something with these items right now. Let yourself reflect on this exercise throughout the remainder of the day.

## AFFIRMATIONS

- I am a person who cares deeply about the people and important memories in my life.

- I hold onto memories in my heart, not in my home.

- My stories do not define me. My memories don't define me. What defines me is what I say about myself.

- I have the clarity to see that every item in my house has a story.

# 5

## You Have a Story. It Doesn't Have You.

At first, Mark couldn't understand why Trent had called him. When Mark met Trent and Jasmine in their living room, their enthusiasm and overt zest for life was abundantly present. Even though they had known each other for several years prior, they had recently married and moved into what was once Jasmine's family's Ft. Lauderdale home. In many ways, they were still in the honeymoon phase of their marriage.

Looking around, the living room was immaculate with plenty of space and wonderful collections of figurines and pottery displayed in curio cabinets. Mark asked if they could give him a tour of the rest of the house. That's when Jasmine piped in with nervous laughter, "No. The rest of the house is off limits."

Trent recalls what happened next:

*Of course we let Mark see the rest of the house. Our kitchen, dining room, guest bedroom, and master bedroom were completely full of furniture—dressers, beds leaning up against the wall, stacks of books, multiple desks with chairs, even the windows were improperly covered with layers of bedsheets.*

*Mark asked, "Whose stuff is this? It doesn't match your living room décor."*

*Jasmine replied, "It belongs to my parents."*

*Mark asked, "Do they live with you?"*

*"No," she said. "They passed away several years ago. This was their home, and mine, too, of course, when I was growing up."*

*I explained that my wife's parents had emigrated from Argentina in the late '50s, moving to the U.S. in an effort to provide opportunities for their two children that apparently didn't exist in their homeland—a good education and a solid career. They had worked very hard their entire lives and were extremely proud of the fact that both Jasmine and her brother, Armond, had obtained college degrees with Jasmine getting her master's degree in education and becoming a school teacher.*

*Mark commented to Jasmine, "It looks like you literally moved your stuff on top of your parents' stuff. There seems to be distinct layers of belongings. The top layer consists of things that you two must have bought more recently. And underneath are the furnishings bought by her parents over the years. Is that accurate?"*

*Jasmine got a little agitated. "Look, Mark. My dad worked for a vending machine company and my mom was a seamstress for a large manufacturer of women's clothing. They came to the U.S. with very little money. They struggled to put me and my brother through college and they sacrificed at every turn. I can't just toss out all of their things after all the effort they put into providing for us." She paused for a moment while chewing on her bottom lip. She crossed her arms and stated, "Neither you nor my husband can make me turn my back on what they did for us."*

## Report the Facts

Let's start with the facts presented by Jasmine's story about her family. It is a fact that her parents emigrated from Argentina in the late '50s. Her dad worked for a vending machine company and her mom was a seamstress for a large manufacturer of women's clothing. They came to the U.S. with very little money. And, it's a fact that Jasmine and her brother graduated from college with financial and emotional support from their parents.

There may be more facts, but these are some we can all agree on.

Let's try this process on one of your stories. Look once again at the chair you described in the last chapter. Reread the story you wrote about how this chair came into your possession and how you chose to place it in this particular room.

After reading it over, we'd like you to list the facts. Only the facts. You can identify the facts by asking yourself questions such as:

What kind of chair is it?

What color?

When did I get the chair?

Did I buy it or did someone else give it to me?

If someone else gave it to me, who was that person?

When did I place it in this room?

What is its intended function?

Make sure you do not include any feelings, assumptions, or added detail that is not strictly fact-based.

_____

_____

_____

_____

_____

## What Is the Story?

Facts, in and of themselves, are rarely very exciting. It's what we make the facts mean to us that engages us and provides us with a well-rounded story. Jasmine had added layers of meaning to the facts about her parents, much like the furnishings layered around her house. She had created a story that was based in feelings, feelings of guilt and misplaced responsibility. Jasmine began to see that when Mark sat down with her and her husband for further conversations. Trent described this experience for us:

*Since our living room was tidy, we had space to sit down together. Mark asked Jasmine, "Do you believe that your parents wanted you and Trent to pile your stuff on top of their things?"*

*Jasmine thought for a moment, then said, "Well, no."*

*Mark continued, "From what you say, your parents created a home that fostered growth and joy. Was there anything that they did or said that would lead you to believe that their desire for you would be to wake up every day, get dressed, and immediately leave the house because it was unlivable?"*

*"Well, of course not."*

*"Was your mother a good cook?"*

*Jasmine nodded, "Oh, yes, some of my best memories are of her cooking in this very same kitchen. But now the kitchen is in such disarray that it's next to impossible to cook there."*

*I added, "We usually go out to eat after work, and take as long as possible before we finally have to go back home and climb into bed. It's not much of a home life."*

*Mark asked Jasmine, "Did your parents ever tell you that they went without something?"*

*"No," she said, "on the contrary, my parents were always happy. Every day was a joy for them, especially when we were together. And in fact, even though they wanted me to become a classical musician, they were completely supportive of me becoming a teacher."*

*"Why?" Mark asked.*

*"I guess they understood that I wanted to make sure everyone has the opportunity to go to school and get educated." Then after a long pause, she added, "Because my parents never had that opportunity."*

*After a moment of silence, Mark responded, "Seeing how your life turned out, I can't imagine that your parents could have been anything but satisfied. I have no doubt they were completely fulfilled."*

*"You're right. They were happy right to the very end."*

The story Jasmine told about her and her family actually imprisoned her and her husband so that they were unable to move forward in their lives. When Jasmine's parents gave her the house, instead of receiving it as a gift and an expression of their love, she saw it as their ultimate sacrifice. As a result, getting rid of her parents' stuff, even though she knew most of it was no longer usable, seemed like an act of disrespect. Jasmine couldn't touch anything without feeling culpable or ungrateful.

Jasmine was the author of this story, one that was rooted in feelings of guilt and misguided responsibility. She had told the story so many times, to herself and others that she honestly didn't know where the facts left off and her own creation started.

Can you identify with Jasmine?

Let's get back to your chair story. Identify the elements you have attributed to the chair that go beyond what the facts have to say. Elements of the story might include:

## *Mark*

Over the years I had collected a number of leather-bound books, most of them dating back to the early 1900s. Without realizing it, the sheer volume of them had soared to over three hundred. It wasn't until I moved that I realized the bulk of them were all stored in my garage. In taking a closer look at why I collected so many, I realized that my love of books was tied to my desire to prove myself academically. Although I had never actually read any of the books, I thought simply by having them they would serve as a sign of my intelligence. On the contrary, there was nothing smart about storing boxes of books. I realized it would be smarter to weed through them, keep the ones that were in perfect condition and in complete sets, and sell off the others. Today, I have books strategically placed throughout my home serving as beautiful accents to the overall décor.

- How you felt about the chair when you first got it.

- If it was a gift, how you felt about the person who gave it to you.

- If you purchased it, what about the chair prompted you to buy it. Did you feel good about the purchase at the time?

- What the chair has come to mean to you over the years.

The story of your chair is comprised of the facts, but so much more. You have endowed the chair with power and significance and meaning that, as a simple piece of furniture, it does not intrinsically possess.

## Identify Your Emotions

The stories that matter to us stir up emotions within us. If your story describes you as a failure, then you will feel like a failure. If your story illustrates that you will never be enough, then you'll go through life feeling inadequate. But if your story affirms you as an empowered and competent person, then you will feel good about yourself and be much more able to address the challenges confronting you.

Let's focus specifically on the feelings your chair story triggers. How do you feel emotionally about the chair itself? Is it your favorite reading chair? Are you delighted to have found the perfect chair to match your kitchen? Is it something you'd secretly like to get rid of, but feel guilty about letting it go? Some of the stories we have attached to our belongings have minimal emotional impact. Others remind us of experiences or people that have caused us a great deal of pain. Take a moment and describe the feelings you experience about the chair. Write these below or in your journal.

_____

_____

_____

_____

_____

Next, notice how your body reacts to this story. We usually consider a memory something that is solely in our minds. But, in fact, memories are stored in our bodies as well as our conscious and unconscious minds. Notice your body as you recall the story. Does your breathing change? Do you feel aches and pains? Are you clenching your teeth, or curling your toes?

Now, rate the intensity of the emotions you feel. When we experience strong emotion, especially more difficult ones, adrenaline and other hormones can be released into our bloodstreams. Our bodies respond as if we're facing danger. The amount of adrenaline released into your bloodstream depends on the intensity of the emotion and sense of distress. The higher the item is rated, the more likely you are to get overwhelmed emotionally and physically. The physical changes occurring inside us can render us unable to think clearly about an object. As long as this item triggers such a strong response, decluttering is nearly impossible.

Using the continuum of 1 to 10, with 1 being motivated, 5 being distracted, and 10 upset and stuck, how would you rate the intensity of the feelings triggered by the chair story?

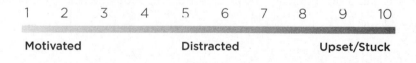

## A Story That Rates a 1 to 3

An item that rates a 1, 2, or 3 triggers little to no intensity, certainly not strong enough to get in your way of making a decision to keep or release an item. When we experience positive or resolved feelings, we are not deterred from taking action. To the contrary, we are motivated to get things in order easily and quickly. One of our goals is to decrease the emotional intensity you experience when telling your story. Once you can rate a story between 1 and 3, you are ready to utilize the strategies in Part Three.

## A Story That Rates a 4 to 7

When feelings intensify to a 4 to 7 level, the stress you are experiencing is strong enough to hinder you from clearing out the clutter and organizing your life, but not so extreme that you are overwhelmed or paralyzed by the memories. This level of emotional intensity often causes you to feel distracted, unmotivated, or unclear about your next objective. You aren't in tears, but you aren't happy either.

One way to assess your stress is to check in with your body. At this point, your brain sends strong hormones like adrenaline into your bloodstream to alert you to danger. Your breathing becomes more rapid and shallow. You may sweat or wiggle nervously. Your mood shifts toward pessimism and your ability to find solutions to your clutter problems will be impaired. It's easy to feel agitated, frustrated, irritable, and short-tempered. It is not healthy, physically or emotionally, to stay in this state for very long.

## A Story That Rates an 8 to 10

If your stress reaches the 8 to 10 level you are experiencing a severe and overwhelming response to a particular story. You may withdraw from the situation and refuse to talk to anyone or you may cling to other people for support. You might have severe physical manifestations such as headaches, sleeplessness, stomach problems, back pain, or panic attacks. You could burst into tears of grief, loneliness, sadness, or have feelings you are unable to identify.

Simply put, you are in crisis mode. We strongly discourage you from trying to deal with a story that is this severely stressful by yourself. Some stories are too traumatic to address alone. These may include stories of childhood abuse, the death of a loved one, an extremely painful divorce, a serious accident, an assault, or a number of other traumatic events. Back away from the story as soon as you can. Calm yourself and take some deep, deep breaths.

We recommend that you talk to someone who is trained in dealing with trauma such as a therapist, body worker, or grief counselor. Stories that rate an 8 to 10 stress level are stories that are holding you back in many areas of your life. Trying to forget them will not work. The memories or symptoms come back to haunt you and deprive you of a future you deserve. At the end of this book we have included some guidelines about how to select a counselor who will be the most effective in helping you address your unresolved trauma.

Before we move from this topic there's one more point we'd like to make. Not all difficult or traumatic experiences will trigger a stress level of 8 to 10. You may have made great strides in dealing with abuse you suffered as a child or as an adult. While the loss of your loved one was extremely painful, you may have been grieving for some time and are ready to make changes in your life. The car accident you suffered, the natural disaster you survived, or the rejection by a loved one might have been overwhelming at the time, but you've made good progress in facing these situations. If this is the case, rate these stories at a lower number.

## You Are the Meaning Maker

In the same way that we made a distinction between you and your house and you and your clutter, we want to accentuate that "you" are not synonymous with your stories. You, as a person, are distinct from the stories you tell about yourself and the feelings these stories trigger. In fact, you are the creator of these stories.

The stories you tell about yourself shape all aspects of your life: your identity, your purpose for being alive, your relationships with other people, your emotional landscape, your spiritual perspective and experience, your political leanings and how you view the world as a whole. It's human nature to attribute meaning to our lives. Every human being is a natural storyteller. Going through life without a clear sense of purpose, worth, or focus can be excruciatingly painful. In fact, it is all but impossible for human beings to live productive, positive lives without finding a reason to get up every morning. We are created with a hunger to make sense of the world as a whole, and for a specific purpose for our individual lives.

Every human being asks the question, "Why am I here?" We answer this personal question through the stories we tell about ourselves and the world around us. Meaning and direction are drawn from different sources—our spiritual beliefs and experiences, our relationships, our life work. Some devote themselves to spiritual disciplines such as prayer, meditation, and movement. Others focus on the study of scriptures and ancient texts. Many gain a sense of purpose through service by helping others in need. Some have a passion for creative expression. There are many ways to explore and express our sense of purpose.

"But wait a minute," you might be saying to yourself, "it's not up to me to 'create' meaning. I don't have that kind of power."

But you do. We all do. Our brains are hardwired to gather information from the world and make sense of it through stories. From infancy onward, we create narratives to help us understand how the world works, how to protect ourselves and how to get what we need and want. You believe your stories, you tell them and perpetuate them, and thus, they shape your world.

You might insist, "My stories are real. Not some made-up fairy tale." Yes, your stories *are* real. They are "real" stories; but real stories can be rewritten to empower you, rather than keep you stuck. A rewritten story can support a great future, not mire you in the past. Why? Because you created them in the first place and you can re-create them.

■ ■ ■

*No matter their source, you believe your stories, you tell them and perpetuate them, and thus, they shape your world.*

■ ■ ■

## Take Back Your Power

Trent continued:

> As Mark and Jasmine looked around at all the things cluttering her space, he asked her, "Are you ready to receive the real gift?"
>     "What would that be?" she asked.

*"Your parents have given you something and you've yet to receive it. It's the opportunity to create your own story, in the same way that they created theirs."*

*It was as if a light went on in Jasmine's mind and heart. "Yes, I can see what you mean." And then my wife did something I had hoped for, but didn't know if I would ever see. Without hesitation, Jasmine got up and started sorting through books.*

*Mark and I looked at each other and then joined her. In a short time, we had the books stacked into piles with a clear sense of what we would do with each pile. And another thing happened that hadn't in a long time. We started joking and laughing and actually having fun! It had been so long since I'd felt anything but dark foreboding when in this house. It started feeling like Jasmine and I were beginning to create our home, rather than live in a mausoleum for her parents.*

With Mark's help, Jasmine and Trent paved a new path, not only to the other rooms in the house, but to their future. The past was no longer a barrier. Nor did they try to deny the past. They honored the past in such a way that they could live in the present and be motivated to action by their commitment to the future.

Do you feel trapped by the stories attached to your clutter? You don't have to.

It is ironic that the thing that can stop us in our tracks is a disempowering story, yet we single-handedly created it. Once we realize that we attribute meaning to our lives through the stories we create and tell, we are no longer held hostage by these stories. We are free to update and revise our stories in light of new information, insight, and enlightenment. Don't allow yourself to be victimized or stymied by the stories you have created. You have the power to address these stories directly in such a way that, once resolved, will rejuvenate you and inspire you to live the life you secretly hope for.

At first this may sound crazy since we know your past is your past and there is nothing we can do to change it. This is true. But you can change the stories you tell about your past. Although some stories might feel so powerful that rewriting them seems impossible. It is possible.

In the next section, we will address these stories, how we create them and how we can easily rewrite them. You're going to be amazed at how much power you have in your life.

## Practices to Live Out, Follow, or Apply

- Look over the ten sticky notes you have created and pick one item that isn't attached to a difficult or intense emotion. It's best to start out with something that has a story that is easy to tell.

- Think for a moment and then list the facts, and only the facts.

- Next tell the story related to this item.

Repeat this process with an item that stirs up emotions rating a 4 to 7.

List the facts, and only the facts.

Think about the story related to this item.

We do not recommend applying this exercise to stories that rate an 8 to 10. If any of your sticky notes merit that high of a stress level, we encourage you to take these off the board. It would be most appropriate for you to explore this story in a safe environment with a friend or a counselor.

## AFFIRMATIONS

- I am who I am. My story is my story.

- I am the creator of all the stories in my life.

- It's safe to be free from my stories because it is safe to be me.

- I have the power to rewrite my stories at any given moment.

- I have the wisdom to create stories that empower me on a daily basis.

# 6

# Be Present to Your Future

Angela was crying the first time Mark came to her house. She told us:

*I was sobbing, sitting in the middle of my living room on top of mountains of clothes, books, and junk that buried my furniture. When I asked Mark to come over to my house and help me, I guess I thought I'd be able to clean up a bit before he actually arrived. You know, so I wouldn't seem THAT bad.*

*I went into the room with a sense of purpose and started sorting through the clothes. I put the dresses in one stack, the blouses in another, and the pants in a third. But it didn't take long until I uncovered the dress I wore at the dance where I met my late husband, and the tears just rolled down my face. I stopped. I couldn't go any further. When Mark arrived and rang the door bell, I hollered through my tears, "Come on in, Mark! I'm in the living room!"*

*Mark came in, surveyed the scene, and then smiled at me. "Here," he said, offering his hand to help me stand up. "Make me a cup of tea and let's go outside on the porch and have a talk."*

*Once seated away from the clutter, Mark asked me, "Angela, forget the clutter for the moment. Don't think about the past or even the present. If anything were possible for your future, what would it be?"*

*I was a bit embarrassed to tell him but he coaxed me. I said, "Not a lot of people in my life now know that I once studied to be a concert pianist. My mother loved music and worked overtime to pay for my piano lessons when I was a little girl. I think I was one of the few kids who actually enjoyed practicing. When I played the piano, it seemed to soothe the stress between my parents. They rarely argued while I was playing. I remember dreaming of being married one day to a wonderful man and having all kinds of music in our home.*

*"I met my husband, Joseph, playing the piano. I was the church pianist and he was the new choir director. We both felt the magic between us the first time we met. We married a few months later, and I've never regretted that decision."*

*Mark asked, "What changed for you?"*

*I explained with tears in my eyes, "I got pregnant right away and had a very difficult time physically and emotionally. I lost that first baby. In fact, I had three miscarriages before I had Isabella. While I was carrying Isabella, my doctor ordered me to bed for nearly seven months. Joseph was a saint. He did all the shopping, cooking, and cleaning. With the hormonal changes, and feeling guilty about having to be in bed all of the time, I fell into a pretty deep depression. Prior to this time, playing the piano had been a source of therapy and creative expression for me. But since I couldn't sit up for any length of time, I was cut off from my music.*

*"I was so relieved when Isabella was born. But I fell back into depression soon after her birth. Those days were really difficult.*

*"Fearing that we'd never have another child, we got pregnant a second time as soon as we could. Once more I was sent to bed. My mother pitched in to care for Isabella while Joseph continued to play husband, father, breadwinner, and homemaker.*

*"After Gregory was born we felt that we had our family. My hands were full with two children and feeling like I owed Joseph so much for his love and hard work. I threw myself into motherhood and homemaking. There simply wasn't time for me to sit down and play the piano."*

*Mark asked me, "But your children are grown. What holds you back now?"*

*I pointed back to the living room. I told him, "On the far corner, over there by the window, is my piano."*

*Mark looked across the room, but there was no piano to be seen.*

*I continued, "It's buried under all that stuff. I have tried repeatedly to get this room under control so that I can dig out the piano. I still dream of playing. Especially now that Joseph has passed away, I'm so lonely at times. The Easter season is coming and I know that the children's choir needs a pianist. But I get so overwhelmed every time I try to tackle the clutter in this room. I don't know what holds me back. Some days I fear that I'll never play the piano again."*

Angela is not the only person we've met who has buried her dreams and talents underneath clutter. Many of the people Mark works with have things they'd like to accomplish, places they want to go, or experiences they would like to have—but can't because their homes are so filled with an unresolved past.

## Every Story Charts Your Future

Our stories are significant, not only because they tell the story of who we are in the present, but because they also lay the foundation of who we will become. This is, perhaps, the most important truth we will share with you in this book. *Your stories, and how you interact with them, will determine your future.*

How can this be? Well, look around your house—it is cluttered with stories. You've got stories stuffed in your closets and jammed into cupboards; stories stacked to the top of your garage and strewn all over your backyard. You've not simply accumulated collectibles, you've collected stories that either contribute to your future or stand in the way of tomorrow's possibilities. Your house is overflowing with items that tell a variety of stories and evoke a variety of feelings. Your living environment either provides space for achieving new goals, or frustrates your efforts. How can you start anything new when there is no room?

*Your stories, and how you interact with them, will determine your future.*

If your belongings could talk, what would they say about you? If your clutter could sing, would all of your belongings sing in harmony like a well-rehearsed choir, or present you with a cacophony of sounds, each clamoring for attention, jockeying to make a point? Do you live in an atmosphere of cohesion or conflict? The sound of clutter can be so distracting that it prevents us from hearing anything else, let alone our true voice from within. The conflict among your stories can add layers of stress to an already overwhelming situation. A sense of spiritual grounding is difficult to experience when surrounded by belongings screaming for attention. It's nearly impossible to live in the present when assaulted by the stories you've attached to your clutter.

Consider this: Talking clutter is not merely a fantasy to consider as an intellectual exercise. Your clutter does speak— loudly and clearly to everyone who enters your home. It speaks of unfulfilled dreams and disappointments, unfinished grief and unexpressed anger. Your clutter reveals your secrets and discloses what you are not willing to acknowledge.

Thoughts often reveal themselves by turning into tangible things. The story of a difficult childhood can appear in the form of a broken doll. Describing yourself as a failure in business can be revealed by piles of unsold merchandise collecting dust in your spare bedroom. Dozens of figurines, some boxed and some peeking out of your cluttered bookshelves, can point to a story that has you frozen in time—as still and cold as they are. The issues in your life

*Your clutter reveals your secrets and discloses what you are not willing to acknowledge.*

you've tried to avoid are sitting right in front of you. Like an unruly child, the Inner "U" is trying to gain your attention one way or the other.

Is it a tragedy that your home isn't perfectly organized? Perhaps not. But if you see that it's a barrier to your future, clutter can be considered a tragedy. Parts of you are tossed, dumped, squashed, and pushed into spaces that are too cramped for creativity. As long as your stories are scattered across the floor and piled up on your couch and spilling from the cabinets, YOU will not be empowered to make positive choices about your future. Instead, the emotional and spiritual chaos you experience will stop you in your tracks.

## If Only . . .

You have a unique purpose in life, a gift to share with the world that only you can give. Darting in and out of your conscious mind, your dreams and desires show themselves, and then hide. What comes to mind when you look over the sea of disorder and sigh, "If only this mess was cleaned up I could . . ."? How do you finish this deep longing? How would you fulfill your potential and make a contribution to the world around you? Here are a few that we've heard people say:

*If only . . .*

. . . I could have the space to set up an in-home gym and get back into shape.

. . . I could create a writing space that was orderly and inspirational so that I could write and tell my story.

. . . I could open a day-care center in my home through which I could express my love for children and have an outlet for my creative energy.

. . . my paperwork would be in order so that I could follow through on some investments I've been interested in exploring.

. . . I could invite small groups into my home where I could offer seminars on oil painting.

Do you have colorful decorations you'd like to display over the holidays? Yes, but . . . you can't find them in the disorder of your extra bedroom. Would you like to invite your loved ones to spend a delightful evening reading aloud from some of your favorite children's books? Yes, but . . . the space by the fireplace is so cluttered no one would have a place to sit. Do you imagine hosting a barbeque next Fourth of July? Yes, but . . . who knows where the grill has ended up? Plus, the backyard is so filled with broken toys and playground equipment that you're too embarrassed to have people over.

Most of us have a sense of what we need and what we have to offer the world. We may not be able to say distinctly, "My purpose is to . . ." but inside you know. We all have dreams of doing extraordinary things with our lives that not only nourish our own souls, but contribute to ourselves, our loved ones, and other people as well.

Listen to yourself whisper your longing when you think no one else will hear. The clutter in your house distracts you from your true self, and from experiencing the highest quality your life has to offer. Up to this point, you have been unable to achieve the quiet and peacefulness needed to hear what your heart wants to say. Instead, your clutter has distracted you, consumed you, agitated you, defeated you. It's impossible to be living in your purpose and potential while stumbling over boxes, desperately searching for your keys, or running out to the store to buy something you know you already have but can't find when you need it. Granted, you might have had moments of contentment and meditation. But unless you are aware of, and hopefully alarmed by, the detrimental impact your clutter has on you, you will not take this opportunity to make a dynamic decision that will impact the rest of your life.

## Your Meaning Makeover

We hope that you haven't stopped dreaming. Most of us have unfulfilled dreams. Some we share out loud and some we try to hide so no one else can laugh at or discourage us. Maybe clutter has become such a way of life for you that hope for this moment and for the future has been buried deep beneath your stuff. We invite you to open yourself up to dreaming again and follow the path of your childlike self with curiosity and whimsy. Approach this with a sense of anticipation for the new things you will discover about yourself; the kind of anticipation that comes just before you open a birthday gift or right before you are about to meet someone special. You shake the gift trying to guess what's inside or you think about how excited you are to see someone after a period of separation. Embrace this genuine feeling that comes from within. This is the voice of the Inner "U." Listen to what you have to say.

We want you to ignore the clutter in your home and explore what you feel you are meant to achieve. If your home is too cluttered, too full of noisy stories yelling out to get your attention, then go to a park or the beach or to a museum. Select a place that both calms you and energizes you. You will uncover your purpose in life, the most accurate sense of meaning, by listening to yourself, not by accumulating excess stuff around you. The quality of your life, not the quantity of things, ultimately is rewarding and affirming. Your home, and all other physical surroundings, will either assist you in fulfilling your purpose, or will get in the way and slow you down.

In order for our external and interior lives to work cooperatively, it is critical that all of our stories tie into our true purpose in life. When we are confronted constantly with stories that are not integrated, walking into one's living room can feel more like being caught in the middle of a screaming match than entering a quiet place to relax or enjoy conversation with friends. The most distracting objects in your home are those that conflict with your authentic self and disrupt your spiritual healing and growth.

The stories we make up about ourselves can be self-fulfilling prophecies. If we say it's going to be a gloomy day, then indeed, it will be a gloomy day. It we think we are a failure, then indeed, we will fail. When we look at the world through a particular lens, such as sadness or discouragement, all we will be able to see is despair and disappointment. Our thoughts and stories shape the world we live in, day in and day out.

Whatever stories you've created about your true passion and purpose will give way to the things in your life, and ultimately how you experience life. But we are willing to bet that you have never fully expressed all of your passions and, more so, brought them to life in a visual way. Now is the time for a meaning makeover.

## Practices to Live Out, Follow, or Apply

The following exercise may be the most significant of any you will complete in this process. We want to help you create *a vision of the future that is so compelling you will make a total commitment to it*. If you skip over this section, or put together a view of the future that is not compelling and energizing, then you will not be motivated to succeed. Doing this section haphazardly will result in nothing more than a list of wants and needs. What's so bad about that? Inadvertently, you will have created an additional barrier to an authentic future. These wants and needs themselves will prevent you from living the life you've always imagined. They will sidetrack you, crowding your inner space (and outer space). As you may have found in your journey so far, focusing on your wants and needs does not move you forward. Wanting and needing will get you more of the same, wanting and needing.

By focusing on the present, by the time you finish this exercise you will have a detailed written description and a visual representation of a future you'll be excited to live. There are three steps involved:

## 1. CONNECT TO YOUR INNER "U"

In each and every moment, you have access to unlimited possibilities. Remember, you are the expert on you. Only you know what kind of future will compel you forward. Be yourself, be present, be the creator of your life, and stand in your future NOW.

Turn your attention to yourself, and to that small voice inside of you that has something life-changing to say. Be present in the moment—*this* moment—in order to envision a future that can contain the person you are meant to be. The only way to access the future is to be present right now. Only when you get oriented to this moment will your future arise and become clear to you.

If it feels difficult for you to gain quietness or focus, try this foolproof way to get yourself into the present: Body awareness anchors us all in the present. Any attention we give to our bodies snaps us out of the past or future and into the present. It's as simple as squeezing your fists then releasing, inhaling and exhaling, or drinking a glass of water. The connection between breath and awareness requires you live in this moment.

Close your eyes and imagine what would be possible if nothing stood in your way. Contemplate the following to stimulate your imagination:

- What talents and gifts are going undeveloped and unshared?

- Are you artistic? Do you want to write? Would you love to garden? Could you be a dynamic public speaker?

- Think about roles you play in life: spouse, parent, sibling, career person. How could you become a more engaged partner if you had time and space to express yourself? Do you wish you were a more involved parent? Have you lost touch with your brothers, sisters, aunts, and uncles? What do you think you could accomplish if you were able to apply yourself in a more focused way on your professional path?

- What do you value in life? Things or relationships? Stuff or accomplishments? Your collections or your contribution to others? Now is the time to be honest with yourself. Are you living true to your values or have you gotten a bit lost?

- Are you clear about your purpose in life? Are you doing the things that are truly meaningful to you? Or are you missing out because you're mired down with a messy house and a heart full of disappointment?

Some people have huge dreams such as starting a charity or a business, new career, or maybe even a family. Others have "smaller" dreams like having time and space to spend playing board games with their kids or having a retreat at home, a place to read. What are the dreams you have for your future? Dreams that in all likelihood won't come to pass as long as your house is full of clutter.

If you get distracted from your visualization, don't be harsh with yourself. Simply turn your attention back to your body and breath. Give yourself all the time and quiet you need to gain clarity. Granted, it is easy to get lost in your stories, like the proverbial "can't see the forest for the trees." When you have trouble accessing the wisdom of your Inner "U," pretend for a moment you had a twin, someone exactly like you. Then ask yourself, "What dreams do I see possible for my twin?" Oddly enough, we give our best advice to others yet we can't seem to listen to ourselves when it comes to challenges in our own lives.

## 2. WRITE DOWN WHAT YOU DISCOVER

You may have multiple dreams of varying sizes or complexities. Write them all down—every last one of them. Take all the time you need. We're not in a hurry. This is one of the most important parts of our journey together.

_____

_____

_____

_____

_____

Next, write down all of the people, besides yourself, that your dreams would help. Would the people living with you have space to fulfill their dreams as well? Would you stop drawing energy from your friends in your current state of despair, freeing them up to explore their talents and gifts? If your dream is to help other people in a direct way, list who would benefit from your efforts. The world, in general, not merely your part of it, would be a better place if you were living out your purpose.

_____

_____

_____

_____

_____

The picture you have in your mind is not merely a dream, it is your purpose unfolding right before your eyes. Your purpose, right now and in each and every moment that will follow, is the blueprint for your future if you allow it to be. You simply need to listen and connect your actions with the message.

After you are finished describing your dreams, imagine that you have already accomplished them. Yes, picture in your mind's eye how you would feel if your dreams were a reality. Proud? Energized? Giddy? Fulfilled? Grateful? Take time to list them all. Then luxuriate in the feelings you would experience if you were able to make your dreams come true. Describe your feelings here or in your journal.

_____

_____

_____

_____

_____

## 3. CREATE A COLLAGE OF YOUR FUTURE

Let your dreams come to life. Create a collage that's true to you! As the picture and feelings become clearer in your mind, create a collage that vividly illustrates your purpose. Bring the words you've written above to life. It may be tempting to skip this step, but remember: If you continue to do the same things, you'll get the same results. It's crucial that you create a vision of your future that is real enough, powerful enough, inspiring enough to motivate you to take a different course of action from this point on. We call this your Purpose Poster.


Create your collage on a piece of poster board by cutting out images from some magazines or printing out photos you have taken. Choose images that represent how you feel, look, and desire to be in this world and in the home. Position and paste them on the board in any manner you see fit. The images can be in black-and-white, full of color, or a mixture of both. They can be large or small, subtle or direct in what they portray. What's most important is that each image represents something about you and the person you know yourself to be, now and in the future. Include at least one picture of yourself in a happy state. Place it in the center of the poster. Do not limit the subject matter solely to images of people however. Use images of objects, places, shapes, colors, even words. As you flip through magazines, if something catches your eye, cut it out and paste it. It caught your attention for a reason and you don't need to know what the reason is. There is no right or wrong way to do this. Do not analyze or edit your process, just go for it. Let your gut reactions and feelings guide you. Take as long as you need to, but try to complete it in one setting.

Once you feel as though it's complete, tape your finished collage on a wall where you can easily see it. Preferably in a room where you spend the most time. This can be in any room in your house. You choose.

- It is safe for me to listen to the voice of my Inner "U" and connect to my inner space.

- Making decisions is easy because I have the clarity of my inner space in which to make them.

- My Inner "U" is abundant and boundless.

- My relationship with myself is improving right now.

- I feel lighter and brighter, calmer and clearer.

# 7

# Sort Your Stories, Not Your Stuff

An airline pilot who has traveled the world many times over, Jorge has collected souvenirs from every place he has flown. When we met him, many of these items were still in their boxes, unopened. In addition to his stash of mementos, Jorge's garage held furniture, boxes of photos, gardening tools, and just plain junk.

Jorge told us:

*I know that Mark has worked with a lot of people with clutter problems, but I think even he was surprised at how many things I was able to get into my garage. My wife, Arianna, is so irritated with me. We just*

*bought her a new car and she wants to be able to park it in the garage.*
*She told me if I didn't have it cleaned out by her deadline, she'd call*
*in an expert. I missed the deadline. The next thing I knew, Mark was*
*here!*

*Mark said, "Don't worry, Jorge. We'll get this garage in order in*
*no time."*

*I liked his optimism but I had one question. "Where do I start?"*

You might be wondering if we're ever going to address the clutter
itself. When will we say, "Okay, now it's time to sort through your stuff?"
Well, we're not quite ready yet. We've still got some of the most important work ahead of us. Where are we going to start? With the stories, of
course! In order to live clutter-free, you need to organize your stories, not
your stuff. Truth is, once you've organized your stories, your belongings
will organize themselves.

In the past, you've been working from a paradigm like the one
below: If you organize your stuff, it will stay organized and you will be
happy.

This would be a perfectly good approach if it caused permanent
change and happiness. But it doesn't. We know what it's like to get caught
in a cycle of defeat and discouragement. Your rooms may be clutter-free
for a brief time, as were ours, but what actually happens is more like
this:

**THE CYCLE OF CLUTTER**
Cluttered Rooms = Source of Unhappiness

Organize
your stuff

Frustration and
Discouragement

You feel happy
temporarily

Clutter
Returns

The heart of traditional clutter-control approaches is the emphasis on "control." The word "control" implies dictating, dominating, and being in charge of your things. If the inanimate objects that comprise the clutter in your home were truly the origin of the problem then perhaps attempting to control your belongings would be effective. However, we believe that there is a spiritual principle at work here. We are not meant to control other people or even things. Instead, we are most power- ful when we create a cooperative relationship with everything around us. Paradoxically, trying to dominate or control something results in a loss of your power. The very thing you try to control ends up tak- ing control of you. Your clutter will, indeed, take over your life. Let's be

## *Carmen*

was the Queen of Clutter Shuffle. I moved piles of stuff from the living room (so we could entertain) to my bedroom (so that I could sort it), then to the garage (so it would be out of the way) and then back to the living room (so I could get to some of the things I wanted to display.) This gave me the illusion that I was making progress on my clutter problem. I suspect I was the only one who was fooled.

honest. You wouldn't be reading this book if you felt able to *control* your clutter.

Our access point to living clutter-free is the process of taking the "U" out of clutter, distinguishing your sense of self from the external chaos around you, and taking responsibility for your stories, not trying to control them. Some stories we can embrace and take with us into the future. Some need to be rewritten, some discarded. We can have an influential relationship with our stories, but we never control them.

Our process utilizes *clutter as an entry point into an exciting process of insight and empowerment* versus a source of unhappiness. This new way of looking at clutter is foundational to the long-term success we've both experienced. We devillainized clutter and addressed the stories that kept us stuck. Once accomplished, the clutter that used to be associated with these stories was easily cleared away. The cycle of clutter had been broken.

Instead of creating a chain reaction of frustration and building unhappiness upon unhappiness, we find ourselves accomplishing our goals and expressing our purpose in life. In the process, we gather more empowering stories. We found it easy to keep up to date on our stories and our clutter, once we understood and cooperated with this dynamic. The diagram below illustrates how our Cycle of Clutter Clarity process works:

**THE CYCLE OF CLUTTER CLARITY**
Cluttered rooms are transformed into a source
of empowerment and clarity

*Organize your
stories*

**Ongoing sense
of purpose and
fulfillment**

*Clutter is
easily sorted
and organized*

*Inspired by a compelling future,
you gain the clarity to clear
clutter and create more
empowering stories*

Sorting our stories is at the heart of the success we've had dealing with the clutter in our lives. We admit to you that this process is an ongoing experience. Our lives keep evolving and growing, bringing change with new challenges and opportunities. The key difference between our approach and those we've all tried before is the capacity to create a flow of energy in our lives. Rather than get mired in piles of clutter, like we used to, we now know to sit down whenever necessary and identify the new stories we have created about our belongings. As we've gotten better at this process, we've not experienced the level of stress we have in the past. In fact, it can even be exciting to sort out our priorities once again, and update the vision we have of our future. This is a process, not a static, one-time decision. And wouldn't life be boring if it wasn't a growing process?

You may find, as we have, that some of your individual stories are thematic. For example, if you have a tendency to feel competitive with your brother, you may have quite a number of stories about how he always won and you always lost or he was the favorite child in the family. There may be the story about the stuffed bear jammed onto the top shelf of your bedroom that reminds you that he got the bigger bear that year at Christmas. The story about the swimming trophy celebrating your second-place win feels like a loss when you remember that your brother came in first. Rather than address the stuffed bear and the trophy through their individual stories, you can combine them and confront the foundational story or issue of low self-esteem all in one. By addressing a thematic storyline of your life, you may be able to rid your heart, and surroundings, of a significant burden.

Whether you address each item individually or in groups of stories with a similar theme, please give yourself permission to sort your stories at a pace that empowers you. It's important that you gain clarity each step of the way and are empowered into the next step in the process. We are not interested in increasing the stress in your life, or encouraging you to address emotionally difficult experiences in a hurried way. We want to share this energizing process with you so that you can get out of the cycle of clutter and experience the calm, confidence and courage available to you.

Borrowing terms that may be familiar to you and are often used in the clutter and design industry, we're going to help you sort your stories into four categories—the four R's:

1. Retain: Stories to keep, just the way they are.

2. Release: Stories that you relinquish, just the way they are.

3. Repurpose: Stories that you update and rewrite.

4. Reserve: Stories you set aside for now after setting a specific deadline to address them.

## Retain: Stories to Keep Just the Way They Are

Jorge continued his story;

*Mark carefully stepped over and between the towers of clutter and picked up a cardboard tube. He pulled the plastic lid from one end and removed a hand-painted canvas. After unrolling it to discover it was a winter scene from Japan, Mark asked, "What is the story of this painting?"*

*I smiled at the memory of our most recent trip to Asia. I told him, "Both Arianna and I love handmade art pieces that are unique to specific areas. We met the man who painted this while walking through the streets of Misawa, in northern Japan. We were both attracted to the grays and blues in the scene. When we stopped to admire the painting, the artist—a small, elderly man—came out of his shop and invited us in to have a cup of tea. He didn't speak much English, and we know only a few words in Japanese, but we communicated easily together about his work. It was an amazing afternoon."*

*Mark asked, "When you bought this painting, did the two of you intend to dump it into the garage?"*

*"Of course not!" I answered. "We have talked about creating a special wall in our living room to showcase this and several other pieces we have from other areas."*

*"What has kept you from doing this?" Mark asked me.*

*I started listing the excuses: "I've got to clean out this garage. We have quite a number of paintings stashed in here. We can't design the display until we have all of them framed and ready to hang up. I know they are in there somewhere."*

We have discovered that there are three critical components to those stories and themes in your life that you intend to keep. In order to retain a story just the way it is, the story must fit all three of the criteria of our Passion Pyramid. A story must 1) promote your purpose, 2) propel your present, and 3) make peace with your past.

## 1. PROMOTE YOUR PURPOSE.

A story to keep, just the way it is, must contribute to achieving the goals you've set for your future. Look at your Purpose Poster. If a particular story or group of stories don't support you, encourage you, or equip you to move forward, then it's time to release, repurpose, or reserve them—they are not stories to keep, just the way they are. To discern if a story promotes your purpose, ask yourself questions such as:

- Does this story, or group of similar stories, motivate or discourage me in moving forward?

- Does this story fit into the vision I have for myself in the future?

- How does this story define who I am becoming? Am I growing in influence or shrinking? Am I becoming a more powerful or weak person? Who am I in terms of achieving my future goals?

- Does this story fit into the vision I have for my future?

- Does this story demonstrate my ability to bring together the resources needed to succeed? Does it illustrate my ongoing ability to problem-solve and learn from experiences?

- Will I be better or less able to fulfill my purpose if I keep this story just the way it is? If the answer is "better able" then it is a story to keep. If the answer is "less able," then set it aside for now. Once we finish this chapter, and you have a clear idea of various options, you can decide where to put this particular story.

Jorge is like many of us—clutter stands in between him and what he most desires for his future. Jorge and Arianna's story about the painting was more than a reminder of a delightful experience they shared in the past. It was a story that reached into their future. Jorge and Arianna have collected a number of treasures in their travels, but have not given themselves permission to fulfill their intentions. Instead, the stories attached to the paintings, as well as the items that represented these stories, were lost somewhere in the sea of clutter in the garage.

Jorge explained:

*Mark asked me if the story of the painting was in line with what Arianna and I wanted to achieve in the future. Without hesitation, I answered, "Yes!" Mark told me that the story had passed the first test required to keep a story just the way it is.*

A story you keep just the way it is is one that fully resonates with your Purpose Poster, the larger story of who you are and who you are becoming.

## 2. PROPEL YOUR PRESENT.

If your story has passed the first test—it promotes your purpose—next, assess whether or not this story propels your present. Your vision of the future is not intended to keep you living in a "someday" mode. It is as much a guide to the way you live out each day in the present as it is to direct you toward the future. We transform our ideas into accomplishments when we engage in actions in the here-and-now that take us in new directions. Before you ask yourself the following questions, take a deep breath, put your shoulders back into a powerful position, and become fully in this present moment. Here are some questions you can ask yourself to determine whether a particular story is to be kept just the way it is:

- Does my body confirm that this is a story to keep by the deep breaths I am taking, the release of stress from my shoulders, or the restful sleep I have at night?

- Does this story motivate me to express my purpose right now? Here? Today?

- Is my creativity sparked by this story? Is my sense of adventure triggered? Is there a smile on my face and hope in my heart?

Jorge realized that the story of the picture brought him into the present moment when he felt the urge to bring Arianna out into the garage to share his discovery. Jorge told us:

*At that moment, I wanted to have Arianna hear what Mark was saying. Prior to this, I was too embarrassed about the garage, and resistant to what she might say in criticism, to include her. I gave her a call, and when she came into the garage, I told her that I felt hopeful for the first time about actually getting our picture display up onto the wall. She beamed at me with a genuine joy. I love seeing her smile like that.*

Stories to keep are useful in the here-and-now, creating new experiences of joy and empowerment. Keep storylines that describe you in terms of success, empowerment, and accomplishment. If a story undermines your confidence or sense of well-being, put it to the side for now.

Let's reflect on Jorge's experience. After gaining encouragement from Mark that he and Arianna could succeed in their dream of displaying their paintings, they were brought fully into the present, no longer stuck in the past or lost in a fantasy about the future.

Assess your story according to the same criteria. Does the story motivate you to stretch yourself, to be the best you can be in each and every moment? You may decide to keep stories about enjoyable traditions and holidays, stories of your family history, or interesting experiences you've had. "Keepers" help you express your spiritual essence, with beauty and inspiration. But if you can't say "yes" to the previous questions, then the story does not support you in the present. A story that burdens you or gets you sidetracked is not one that is to be kept just the way it is.

Jorge continued:

> *After Mark and I discussed the picture for a while, he suggested that I put the painting in my car so that Arianna and I could get it framed next time we were out. I thought, "Well, of course!" Now I'm actually looking forward to getting things sorted out in the garage so I can locate the other pieces we want to display. I'm feeling so much more energized than I did before about this garage project.*

### 3. MAKES PEACE WITH YOUR PAST.

The third side of our Passion Pyramid refers to whether or not you have a sense of well-being when telling a story. Are you at peace with this story or does it trigger feelings of distress? How intense are these feelings? Easy to deal with or overwhelming?

What does this story contribute to your life? There are at least two ways of viewing your past "mistakes"— as blunders or as learning experiences, as failures or means of gaining wisdom. A story to keep just the way it is speaks of ways you have developed your gifts and talents, not about how you squandered opportunities.

For example, imagine that in the past you were tricked by a friend and lost money in the process. Is this the story about how bad you are at judging another person's character or is it about how you have learned to take seriously the "red flags" in the behavior of people before you trust? Does the story tell about how foolishly you've handled money or what you have learned about managing money? The facts in both stories may be the same, but the focus and the meaning of the story are different. The first version of your money management triggers feelings of shame and discouragement, and defines you as a victim. In contrast, the second version increases your credibility and confidence to deal with difficulty.

Ask yourself questions such as:

- Do my shoulders (fists, jaw, stomach) tighten up when I recall this story? Or am I relaxed?

- Do I enjoy telling the story or do I wish I could avoid sharing this story with others?

- Am I genuinely at peace with this part of my past? If not, then do not keep it just the way it is.

Only keep a story if it is affirming. If you feel shamed or your confidence undermined, put it aside for now. As we move through the other categories, you may find just the right fit.

Remember, the future you have represented in your Purpose Poster is designed to motivate you to do the sometimes difficult work of sorting your stories. If the images and words on the poster do not inspire you to action, then your sense of purpose is not fully expressed or represented. If that is the case, we encourage you to return to the previous chapter and add to creating a compelling picture of your sense of purpose.

Seeing a future that gives your life meaning and directs your activities toward significant goals is essential to creating a living space that makes it possible to succeed. Stories that need to be discarded or rewritten tend to drain the vitality from us. When trying to decide whether or not a particular story is best kept just the way it is, notice how you respond to the story emotionally. If you feel motivated to move forward, it's probably a story that supports and contributes to your future dreams and ambitions. Check in with your body. If you're still holding your breath or clenching your jaw, or you have a slight headache or your back muscles are tense then the story may fall into our next category.

## Release: Stories to Relinquish Just the Way They Are

As we've discussed in the previous section, some of the stories we tell about ourselves do not contribute to our lives in any helpful way. They serve no positive purpose. You may realize that a story you've told for years is no longer relevant, or that it describes a situation that no longer exists. Perhaps the story communicates an attitude that holds you back. These stories are best identified and discarded just the way they are.

* * *

Jorge had a few stories like that.

*Mark opened up a large box that has been sitting in our garage for several years. Inside were outdated calendars, receipt books, envelopes, and other items for a business I started several years ago. I told Mark, "I thought I'd be good at importing handmade calendars I discovered in Thailand. But it was pretty much a disaster. I couldn't sell them fast enough. Before long, I had stacks of outdated calendars. They were beautifully made, but no longer sellable. So, all of it got thrown into boxes and stored down here."*

*Mark asked, "How does the story of these items contribute to your future?"*

*I told him, "It doesn't, actually. Whenever I come across this box, and there are a few more in here somewhere, I feel tired. I really put a lot of effort into this project. But I came away from the experience feeling discouraged. At least we learned that I was not cut out for the importing business."*

*Mark asked, "Did that information help you make other decisions?"*

*I sighed and said, "Yes. I thought I could retire early from the airlines if I could make a go of this business. But through this I realized that I needed to keep flying. Now I'm really glad I did because I met Arianna soon after that while touring the Middle East. If I'd left the airlines, I wouldn't have been on that trip and would have never met her."*

*Mark asked me, "Do you need to keep the story of your failed importing business?"*

*I responded, "No, I guess not. I'm not a failure. I'm a really good pilot. It's not a story that contributes to my life. I can see now that I don't need that story at all."*

If letting go of a story breathes new life into your bones and a lightness of heart, then it's a story that can be relinquished in its entirety. A story to be discarded, just the way it is, will be relatively easy to toss out once you take some time to assess its nature. If a story makes you feel weary, let it go. Stop telling the story—to yourself or anyone else. If you are belittled or described in ways that are outdated, let the story go. If you no longer can make use of the story, let it go. There is no reason to tell this story ever again. It has no place in your life today or in your future.

What do you do if you try to let go of a story, but it simply won't leave? You know it describes you in outdated terms, or tells of an experience you thought you had resolved. If you find that the story comes back, creeping into your mind, then take note of this dynamic. When it's extremely difficult, or nearly impossible to let a story go, it may fall into the next category we're going to discuss.

## Repurpose: Stories to Be Updated and Rewritten

Some of your stories will not fit into the two categories we've discussed so far. They may not fully support your present or future, nor are you ready to fully release them either. These are stories that point to unfinished business, unspoken words of forgiveness, or incomplete intentions. Before you can put some stories in your "Keep or Discard Just the Way They Are" categories, they need to be rewritten. A story that distracts you, drains your motivation, or gets you going off in some unhelpful direction is one that calls to be rewritten.

We're not suggesting that you make up new facts about your life, or ignore the reality of your past. We don't want to promote denial and self-delusion. In fact, the contrary is true. Ignoring significant and shaping past experiences will keep you tied to these stories, and stuck in your clutter. Unless a story is truly resolved, you will not be completely free of its impact. As a matter of fact, the clutter all around you is the result of avoiding unpleasant stories that tell of very real, influential, and often painful occurrences in your past.

You may have tried to banish these stories by thinking more positively about yourself. We've tried that approach, but relying on "positive thinking" alone did not work for us. First of all, it's impossible to think *only* of positive things. As soon as you say, "I'm going to be positive," you *must* imagine its opposite—the negative in your life. In the same way that you can't think about "up" without thinking of "down," or you can't describe the weather as "cold" without comparing it to your experience of "hot." You can't think positive thoughts without comparing them to the negative.

*The clutter all around you is the result of avoiding unpleasant stories.*

Secondly, while thoughts are important, they are insufficient in turning yourself toward success. While we need to be optimistic about what we can accomplish, we believe that thoughts alone, without accompanying actions, will not empower us for positive change. Instead of merely "thinking" positive thoughts, you are capable of "living" positively as you transform the hurtful experiences in your life into stories that speak of hope, competency, second chances, fulfilled dreams, and deepening, fulfilling relationships.

Why do we believe that you have the power to rewrite stories? At some time in your past, you wrote the stories to begin with. You are the *only* one who can reshape those stories that block the path to a positive future because you are the author of the story in the first place.

How do you know if you're ready to rewrite a story? On the stress continuum, a story that is ready to be revised will fall between 1 and 6 on the stress scale. If a story rates a 1, 2, or 3, you'll find it relatively easy to revise the story. You may experience a bit of embarrassment, but nothing that shames you into inaction. There may be some apprehension, but not full-blown fear. There may be a hint of irritation or annoyance, but not outrage. A story between 1 and 3 needs a bit of tweaking in order to keep it, but not a major overhaul.

> *You are the only one who can reshape those stories that block the path to a positive future because you are the author of the story in the first place.*

If a story rates somewhere between 4 and 7, it will require more thought and focus. You may experience some embarrassment or shame. You may suffer from guilt or remorse, or fear and anger. A number of feelings may be triggered by this story, but it isn't the nature of the emotions that is significant—it is the intensity of these feelings that will let you know if it's a story you can rewrite at this time.

## Andrew and Carrie's Story

Even though they had gotten along extremely well while they were dating, now that Andrew and Carrie were married, they argued all the time. Carrie had moved into Andrew's home, but, according to Carrie, Andrew had never made enough space for her to feel at home. The one item that caused the most friction was the huge waterbed in their bedroom. Carrie told me, "There's no room for anything but the bed! It's massive. I want us to get a bed that fits nicely into the room and get a bureau and maybe a chair."

Andrew made it clear that he was very attached to the waterbed. He said, "Mark, I love that waterbed. I've had it for years. In fact I got it right after I graduated from college. I don't see why we should spend money on a new bed when this one is here and great to sleep in."

Carrie was also unhappy with the backyard. We all walked to the backyard to see what could be done. I asked Andrew to describe what he saw . . . just the facts.

Andrew said, "I see a hot tub, a basketball hoop, a barbecue, a Ping-Pong table, and my old Kegerator."

Next I asked him to tell the story of the backyard. Andrew told me, "Well, I used to play basketball with my buddies from college, but I rarely play now. I know Carrie would like to entertain, but I don't want to spend the money on a new barbecue. Granted, my old one here has rusted up pretty badly."

I asked, "When was the last time you and Carrie played Ping-Pong?"

Carrie and Andrew both laughed. Carrie said, "Mark, we've never played Ping-Pong together. Nothing back here is of interest to me. Maybe the hot tub would be fun if it was cleaned and the water was maintained. But the rest of it, well . . ."

Andrew began to see that all of the things around the backyard were "his," not "theirs." Andrew admitted, "I feel a little panicked when I think of letting all of this go."

"You've made a big change in your life," I told Andrew. "I can imagine moving from being a single man to a married man can be stressful, even though it is something you want."

Andrew nodded his head and said, "Yes, it's been harder than I expected." He put his arm around Carrie. "Don't get me wrong, I love Carrie with all of my heart. She's not the problem. It feels like I'm losing a really important part of myself if I let these go."

Andrew fell head over heels for Carrie and vowed to love her, and grow old with her. However, it was clear to all of us that Andrew had yet to make way for his new bride. Without really paying attention, he thought a waterbed would be appropriate for them. Carrie made it very clear that she felt very uncomfortable in it.

Andrew needed to rewrite the story surrounding his identity to make room for what mattered most to him—his relationship with his wife. He now had someone else to think about. It was time to redefine his old ways.

After some time working together, Andrew rewrote his story. He said, "I want to be the best husband I can be and to continue creating my identity inside my relationship as a husband, friend, and partner. I am committed to having things in my home that reflect me and my wife's taste, especially when it comes to things we share, like a bed."

To Carrie's delight, Andrew gave the waterbed to his younger brother, who thought it was the next best thing since sliced bread. Carrie and Andrew, together, picked out a new bedroom set, making room for their future.

The new story you create out of the facts may call for some action on your part. As you see the past from a new perspective, you may find the need to apologize for things you did or said in the past. You may need to take responsibility and make amends. Or you may need to tell a friend or family member how you were hurt by something that occurred between you. Since stories have power, a rewrite will exert new energy in your life, calling you to a change in self-perception and to clearer, more functional relationships.

Let's return to Jorge for a moment to see how this occurred for him.

*Mark dug a bit deeper into the boxes of calendars and found some handmade stationery. Mark said, "These items aren't time-bound like the calendars. What is their story?"*

*I told him that the same women who created the calendars also made stationery using a bush that grew in their area. They pruned the bushes each year and made paper out of the cuttings. I hadn't remembered how amazing these paper products are.*

*Mark asked, "When you see these stationery sets, what do you feel?"*

*I thought for a moment and said, "They trigger the same feelings of failure the calendars do, except that I don't have the same desire to discard them. It's a shame to toss such beautiful creations."*

*"You can rewrite the story if you choose," Mark told me.*

*"How do I do that?" I asked.*

*He said, "You can change what the stationery means, and its function in your life, by writing a new story. For example, the story could be that you collected some beautiful items in your travels and you are going to use the stationery yourself, or give the sets as gifts to friends and family. There is no mandate for you to associate them with your failed business."*

*It was so liberating to be empowered like this. "Oh, that's a great idea. I don't think I've ever shown them to Arianna because I packed all that stuff away before I met her. I'll bet she will love these," I said*

*as I pulled the packets out of the box. "Yes, Mark, you've really helped
me see that I am only a failure if I choose to define myself in negative
terms. I have the power to write and rewrite my own stories."*

The story Jorge rewrote gave him an opportunity to view himself
in a more accurate and positive light, with the added benefit of giving
to others. No longer would the stationery conjure up a story of failure.
To the contrary, Jorge was free to tell the inspirational stories about
the stationery—the women who created sellable paper products. Telling their stories could increase the awareness of the plight of women in
developing countries among his friends and family members. Perhaps
someone who received a stationery set as a gift would be drawn to helping these women. No one knows what can come out of telling our own
truth in a way that bolsters creativity and caring. Like dominoes set in
motion, when we rewrite our stories a myriad of unexpected and wonderful things can occur as a result.

But what about stories that cause you significant stress? Stories that
warrant an 8 to 10 on the stress continuum are to be set aside. We will
also take a look at these stories.

## Reserve: Stories You Set Side for Now After
## Setting a Specific Deadline to Address Them

We believe there are two legitimate reasons for putting stories into the
Reserve category. First, if you are facing layers and layers of clutter, you
are also facing layers and layers of stories. Taking on an entire house of
stories might be a bit much for one afternoon. If you are like Jorge and
have accumulated an enormous pile of stories in and around your home,

it's not practical to try to sort them all today. We know from firsthand experience that it's all but impossible to sort through all of your stories at once. As we've said before, this is a process and pacing is important.

Consider grouping stories into themes when you feel engulfed by the sheer volume of clutter and attached stories. You may discover that an entire room conveys the same story—it might be cluttered with childhood memories or a disarray of paperwork. Instead of addressing the story of each toy or piece of paper individually, it can be helpful and more time efficient to address the thematic storylines. You may find that it is easier to confront the theme of unresolved experiences than it is to confront individual stories. However, beware of the "clutter shuffle." You don't get any points for merely moving your stories around like chess pieces.

As long as you don't use this category as an avoidance technique, setting some stories aside can help you move forward rather than becoming overwhelmed and stymied altogether. Only you know what your real intentions are—avoidance or pacing. You are acting with integrity if you are actively addressing your stories one at a time, with the expectation of taking on a new story once the current story has been released or rewritten.

Second, this category is also where extremely difficult stories ought to be placed. If a story rates an 8 to 10, then it is not wise to address it quickly or by yourself. A story that triggers intense emotion deserves significant processing and exploration. Perhaps these are the most important stories in your life—so crucial and powerful that they can stop you in your tracks. Addressing and disempowering these stories is essential to actualizing the future you have envisioned.

If a story evokes intense and painful emotions, or if you find that it's difficult to recall certain aspects of the story, then we strongly encourage you to get needed support and assistance. We know that some people have had harrowing things happen to them, suffering great loss or tragedy. We do not want to make light of these experiences as if they are easy to discard or rewrite. If you have been abused or misused in some way, we urge you to confront these stories at the appropriate time with ample support. Moving forward at an effective speed that displays self-respect is essential. You will make no progress, and might even compound the hurt you've experienced in the past, if you take on these stories hastily or without needed assistance. Please read over our recommendations for locating a therapist or support group on page 257.

## Practices to Live Out, Follow, or Apply

- You live in your house, but reside in your inner space. When you feel overwhelmed or distracted, take a moment to get reacquainted with yourself. What excites you? What makes you giddy? What lights you up? What makes you smile? What does your future look like? If your external world creeps in, recognize that it's out of date. It's not the present you.

- For this next exercise, you will need sticky notes and a pen. Select one area in your house that you consider "cluttered." Pick five items that you consider a part of the clutter and write down the excuse you tell yourself for why it's a part of your clutter and you're not getting the space organized. For example:

"I might need this one day"

"I can't give this up, I'd feel too guilty."

"I've had this since I was a child."

"This is part of a collection I have."

Now take the sticky note and attach it to each item.

AFFIRMATIONS

- I feel free, calm, and peaceful and am moving on with my life.

- Life is easier because I am easier on myself.

- I am kinder to myself when I am kinder to my space, both inner space and outer space.

- There's only one of me. I give thanks for that.

- How will life surprise me today? I am open to the *present* life is offering.

## Part One: In Review

Before we tackle the next major step, let's review the points and progress we have made so far:

1. You are the expert on your life.

2. You have been party to every decision that has taken place in your house, either directly or indirectly.

3. Your house is your house and you are you—two distinct entities.

4. You can put a price tag on your house, but not on you.

5. You are a natural-born storyteller. It's part of being human.

6. You attach a story to every item in your house.

7. You are relating to the story of each item, not the item itself.

8. You have the power to change each story since you are the creator of it.

9. You are clear about your present purpose and have a vision of your future

In addition, we've started outlining a process to deal with your stories, a process that we will explore more deeply in the next section.

In the next section, we will take a look at some of the most common excuses people—ourselves included—use to avoid dealing with their clutter.

Before people recognize that their stories, not their clutter, hold them back, we usually hear a litany of excuses for the clutter around their homes. It's easy to come up with excuses when perplexed by the inability to live clutter-free. Most so-called experts will encourage you to stop complaining and get on with it. Sell it at the yard sale! Give it to charity! Toss it in the trash! Stop with the excuses, already!

But wait. We believe that "excuses" are actually clues to the underlying issues at hand. We've noticed a few things about most of the excuses we hear. Making excuses, rather than taking action, can pay off in the short run. A phrase like "I'd love to get organized but I don't have time" is an excuse many of us have used. The payoff? We get to do other things we'd prefer rather than confront the clutter. It's a great way to avoid taking responsibility for our choices and a great way to justify our self-destructive behavior.

Even though an excuse may come in handy at any given moment, there are dire consequences in the long run. Simply stated: *Excuses result in the stifling of our dreams.* An excuse like "I don't know where to start" disempowers us. We tell ourselves and others that we are incompetent, helpless, and overwhelmed. Our bodies are drained of energy and our hearts of optimism. When we live neck-deep in clutter, we suffer consequences that can be extremely painful, such as missing the opportunity to spend time with your family or to launch a new home business. We sacrifice long-term happiness and fulfillment, and our skills and talents are not developed.

If this is true, then it begs the question: *Why do we keep using excuses for not getting organized?* Doesn't it make more sense to embrace your talents and passions for the future? We believe that the excuses we give are messages from your Inner "U." Think of this as receiving a letter written in a secret code that you must decipher to understand. Once you break the code and the message is revealed, you will experience clarity and power you've not had before.

As we start reviewing the five most common clutter-avoidance excuses, we request that you look to see if you can identify and find yourself in these examples. In our experience, most people use one, two, or all of these excuses depending on what items we are talking about. You may have a slightly different expression of the excuse, but bottom line, they all come from the same place—living amidst unsorted stories that have the power to keep us from our purpose in life. It's time to *listen* to yourself, your Inner "U," to discover a message that will change your life. What you are saying through these stories is vitally important and holds the key to moving forward.

Part Two

# Stories That Hold Us All Back

# 8

# Excuse #1: "I might need this someday."

Stacie told us that she just couldn't seem to let go of the scrapbooking materials she'd collected over the years:

*I'll be honest. The garage and the guest room are packed with boxes filled with photos, scrapbooks, stickers, and other paraphernalia. I've even got some boxes in my bedroom. Mark told me that the garage was a giant scrapbook gone wrong.*

*I remember being pretty defensive at the time. I told him, "I need all of this stuff!" I was not going to toss all of my supplies just to make Mark happy. I insisted, "Mark, I am going to use all of these supplies someday. When I do, I don't want to have to go out and buy all of this again. Plus," I said, "money is so scarce right now. With my husband unemployed, I am supporting all of us on my part-time job. I can't waste money that way."*

## The Fear of Scarcity

We live at a unique time in history. Highly educated people, well-versed in economics, are scrambling for paradigms that will help us explain and cope with the abrupt and often unpredictable changes occurring in the world's economy. It's enough to scare anyone.

Nevertheless, the fear of scarcity is nothing new. Rooted in a faulty belief system, the fear of scarcity promotes the idea that if we hoard what we have right now, we won't go without in the future. That's simply not true. *Clutter does not protect you in the future—it blocks you* from *your future.*

> *Clutter does not protect you in the future—it blocks you from your future.*

Let us ask you a question. "Do you feel financially secure right now?"

Let's assume you answered "yes" to this question. Think about the basis upon which you feel confident in your finances. Take a moment and identify what you have in place to provide for you and your family in the future. Please write these down here or in your journal.

_____

_____

_____

Now look at what you have written. Perhaps you mentioned your savings account, or investments that will provide for you and your family in the days to come. You are capable of this achievement—a plan of action that supports your sense of security.

Look again at the list. Did you write, "I feel financially secure because I have a house full of clutter?" Probably not. Don't get us wrong. We are not advising against having supplies on hand that might be of use in the event of a natural disaster or other major crisis. It is wise to be prepared, having items your family might need—supplies that are organized and easily accessible. But your family won't be better equipped to deal with a crisis because you have stockpiled jars of nails, bolts of cloth, outdated clothing, or dozens of shoes. Your clutter will slow you down, not assist you, in responding effectively to the challenges ahead.

Let's look at the issues if you answered "no" to the question "Do you feel financially secure right now?" The possessions you have right now do not provide a sense of well-being or security. At this moment in time, with your house filled to the brim with stuff, you feel insecure. There is no basis for thinking that this stuff will be of any help to you in the future.

Hoarding clutter has already proven itself as a failed strategy. You can keep every single item you currently own for the rest of your life, and still not experience a sense of financial security. Clinging to all of these objects won't change how frightened you feel, or provide for your genuine financial needs.

* * *

Stacie continued with her story:

*Mark pointed out to me that I had already spent a lot of money on these items. He said, "Stacie, the money is already gone."*

*I just stared at him, so he kept pounding the point home. "The money has already been spent. You can't get it back no matter what you do with these things. How will storing all of this stuff get your money back?"*

*"Well," I told him, "I guess it can't get the money back. But I could use these supplies and then I wouldn't have wasted my money."*

*Mark responded, "That may be true. But I'm responding to your excuse—that confronting this clutter would result in a waste of money. Keeping these items now won't change the fact that the money has already been spent."*

*I took this in and then said, "So you think I'm just using this as an excuse, right?"*

*Mark said, "Ultimately, it's not important what I think. It's what you think. But I'd like to ask you a few more questions. Let's imagine that you decided to dedicate the rest of the day to scrapbooking. Which scrapbook would you select to work on?"*

*I thought for a moment and responded, "Mark, I have no idea which scrapbook I was working on or where it could be in this pile."*

*Mark responded, "Then what about beginning a new project with a new book?"*

*I smiled. "Okay, Mark. You've made your point. It would take days and days of sorting and reorganizing to get all of these supplies in working order. I could not, in one afternoon, begin a new project, find the appropriate photos, and locate the stickers, pens, and glue I'd need."*

*Mark asked, "Do you believe you are using all of this as a cover-up for moving ahead with your life?"*

*I gave out a big sigh. "Yes, I believe I am."*

## Report the Facts

We've observed that most of the people who struggle with a sense of scarcity have a lot of belongings. Rather than have one antique dresser, they have rooms full of bedroom furniture. Rather than have an adequate amount of office supplies for their home office, they fill up their houses with all kinds of paper, rubber bands, paper clips, and office décor. The motto is: If one is good, a lot is much better. Having a single item is never enough for those of us who are frightened of not having what we need some time in the future. What one person accumulates might differ from what another might collect, but we all share an irrational fear of going without—and attach that fear to our belongings.

Are you like this as well? You might have an abundance of hardware, glass bottles, or cooking utensils. Perhaps you hoard picture frames, old hats, or Hummels. It doesn't matter what we hoard; it's that we do this for the purpose of covering up our fear of scarcity.

Select something you have kept for the purpose of making you feel safer financially. Pick something you keep because parting with it would seem like a waste of money. Now describe it . . . just the facts.

What is it? What color is it? When did you get it? Where and how did you get this? How did it come to be in the place it is right now?

_____

_____

_____

_____

_____

Mark walked Stacie through the same exercise. Stacie told us:

> *Mark asked me to list the facts about my scrapbooking supplies. I said, "Well, I started scrapbooking when I found out I was pregnant with Teddy. He's fifteen now, so it's been quite a few years. I used to attend conferences and classes on scrapbooking to learn new ways of creating pages. Each time I went, I bought more supplies."*
>
> *Mark asked, "About how many blank scrapbooking pages do you have here?"*
>
> *Oh, I couldn't count them! I admitted, "I have hundreds of pages. All kinds of stickers, hole punches with different designs, tools, different kinds of glues . . . There is several thousand dollars' worth of supplies here. And boxes and boxes of unorganized photos."*

## Tell the Story

Now it's time to tell the story. This was Stacie's story:

*All of these supplies revolve around my son, and creating positive memories for him. I was the fifth child of a large family and no one ever saved pictures of my childhood. I wanted it to be different for my son.*

*When I started scrapbooking, my husband thought it was a great idea, at least at first. He liked taking pictures and I enjoyed creating the pages. It was something we did together—a real family thing. I envisioned us all working on these together over the years.*

*But once Teddy was born, he was so sick at first, I didn't have the time or energy to keep up the pace. My husband kept taking pictures, but I never caught up. He's always enjoyed photography, but now it's not something we share as a family. He knows that all of the photos he takes of the family, especially the ones of Teddy, will end up stashed in the garage.*

Now it's your turn. What is the story of the item you selected? Write out the story in detail.

_____

_____

_____

_____

_____

## Identify Your Feelings

List the feelings that you associate with this item. Please complete this part of the exercise before you read further.

_____

_____

_____

If a fear of scarcity is at the root of your clutter collecting, you'll find it on the list you just made. It might have been expressed in a variety of ways, such as "I feel guilty about wasting all of this money" or "I feel pressured to make use of these items in order to be responsible financially." You may state your fear of scarcity in other words. Take a look at what you wrote to see if this fear is something you experience.

Stacie discovered that she had strong feelings about her stash of supplies. She recalled:

> *I told Mark, "When I look at these boxes, I feel sad about the opportu-nities I've lost to create something with my husband and son. Teddy is*

*growing up so fast and I feel so badly that I haven't done this for him. And I feel ashamed about how I've treated my husband's photos too. I feel frustrated that I can't get to the boxes when I need something so I don't move ahead with a project. I'd have to go out and buy more supplies since I can't find what I need. I feel too guilty about spending any more money, so I just get stuck. I've wasted a lot of opportunities and money. I feel pretty badly about it."*

*Mark summarized, "So you feel sad and wasteful. Is that right?"*

*I nodded and admitted, "Yes, that's exactly how I feel. I've wasted money and I've lost opportunities I can never get back. I'm afraid that if I give all of this up, I'll never be able to afford these items again."*

## Assess Your Stress

Now, on a from 1 to 10 scale, with 1 being motivated to move forward and 10 being stuck and overwhelmed, how would you rate the intensity of the fear that you experience? Imagine yourself sorting through your clutter. Notice your body. Are you breathing deeply or shallowly? Perhaps you are not breathing at all. Are you shaking your foot with nervousness? Chewing your lip? Do tears come to your eyes? Your body will let you know the level of your stress.

Most of us are easily detoured by unpleasant feelings. Stacie was no different.

Stacie rated the intensity of her feelings at 7. She told us:

*This is a huge source of distress in my life. My husband feels that I don't value the pictures he's taken over the years. I don't know if Teddy minds it much, but I feel like I have let him down. So, yes, it is like a weight I carry on my shoulders all the time. Each time I try to get a handle on this, I find myself in tears. I just go inside the house and do something else.*

Write down the number that represents your stress level on a sticky note and attach it to the object in question.

## Be Present to Your Future

Stacie continued with her story:

*While I was confessing all of this to Mark, Teddy walked up to us and eyed the garage. He said, "Mom!" Actually he said the word "mom" as if it were two syllables . . . "Maa—ummm. When are you going to get rid of all this junk? You know my band needs a place to practice. There's no room in here for us."*

*I looked at Mark red-faced. "I guess Teddy does have feelings about this garage. He wants me to make room for him to practice with his band."*

*Mark asked, "How does it feel knowing that your son has no place to pursue his love of music?"*

*"It adds to my stress," I told him.*

*Mark looked around and then asked me, "What will the story of your family be if you keep things exactly the way they are? Will you sacrifice all of the future opportunities to create a home where your son and his friends like to spend their time, because you feel so badly about other opportunities you've lost? Are you going to waste the future because you feel badly about the past?"*

*I had never thought if it that way. It didn't make any sense to keep all of this stuff if it was depriving us of being a family. Mark asked me, "Wouldn't you prefer to have Teddy home with his friends, where you and your husband can enjoy and keep an eye on him, rather than out somewhere?"*

*I responded, "Of course, I would." And then I let it all sink in. "I can see I need to face my fears and choose something new and positive that will happen—if I make room for it." Then I got stuck again: "But I don't want to just give it away!"*

*Mark laughed. "I haven't said one word about what to do with all of these supplies. We don't have to figure that out in order for you to decide that you are going to do SOMETHING with them."*

*I saw that my desire to keep these supplies stemmed from my fear that I may not be able to afford them one day, and also guilt over what I hadn't achieved in the past. But actually, I had bigger issues with money. I was ready to admit to myself that I hadn't been spending money wisely. I so desperately wanted to hold onto my son's childhood memories inside the pages of the scrapbooks I was going to make someday that I was depriving us all of new opportunities.*

Ask yourself similar questions:

- What are you wasting in an effort to feel safe?

- What are you hoarding to avoid facing the past and committing to a brighter future?

- Does hoarding items contribute to your financial and experiential wealth? Or does it cost you much more than these items are worth to you?

Take some time to imagine what your life would be like if all of this clutter was removed. Now, make the decision—right now—to do something with your clutter. You don't have to decide *what* to do with it before you decide to do *something* with it. Just make the decision to go down a different path. Exactly what will become of your story will be determined in the next section. For now, making a decision to do something will help you move forward. Later in this book we're going to help you create strategies to clear out the clutter itself. But nowhere in this book will we tell you what you "should" do with your clutter. We're going to assist you in figuring out your own strategy, one that will work just for you.

In the meantime, you have new information about yourself. Now that you've discovered that you have a problem with using your money and time wisely, something that also takes away from your relationships and creating future memories, you are free to focus on your real issues. The problem is not going to be solved by focusing on your clutter. Clutter is extremely costly—it wastes our energy, undermines our relationships, and gobbles up our time. Once you recognize that your fear of scarcity will not contribute to your life in any way, you will make room for activities and items that can provide for you in the future. The things you have squirreled away are pointing you to the underlying issue, and at the same time, the opportunity for abundance.

## Sort Your Stories

As we said earlier, your story can be sorted in one of four categories: 1) Keep it just the way it is, 2) Release it just the way it is, 3) Rewrite it, or 4) Reserve this story to be resolved at a later date.

Mark asked Stacie if she wanted to keep this story just the way it was. Stacie told us:

*When Mark suggested I keep things like they are, I immediately said, "No way! I'm ready for a change."*

*Mark asked me, "Are you ready to release this story, just the way it is?"*

*I said, "No, I'm not ready for that either. Granted this story is about wasting money and valuable opportunities. But it is also about the desire to create a shared experience for all members of my family."*

*"So, do you want to rewrite it?" Mark asked. I said I would like that. Mark continued, "You rated your story as a 7 on the stress continuum. That's pretty high. Do you need more support than I'm offering to deal with this?"*

*I told him that he gave me all the support I needed.*

*Mark observed, "You want to keep the part of the story that values family, right?" I nodded and he continued, "The story of family is one you are ready to keep, just as it is. The part that you want to rewrite is about amassing the photos and the scrapbooking supplies."*

*I told him, "I don't want to get rid of the photos. These are pictures of us as a family. That fits into the part of the story I want to keep."*

*Mark asked, "What feelings do you associate with those photos right now?"*

*I thought for a while and then responded, "I feel like I've let my family, especially my husband, down by not putting them in scrapbooks where we can enjoy them. And that brings me back to where I started."*

"Is putting them in scrapbooks the only way you can enjoy them?" Mark asked.

I hadn't thought about that before. I gave it a little more thought. "Actually, I could pick up some photo boxes and sort them according to date. That would go relatively quickly."

Mark added, "And this could be a project that your husband or son might want to do with you."

I smiled. "That sounds really fun. I'd love to do that."

Mark pointed out, "I want you to notice how much energy you are feeling now that you have rewritten the story. You now have a story that serves your goals for the future—to have more family time doing things you all enjoy."

I really love this process!

Mark then said, "Okay, there is one last part of the story that needs to be addressed. The scrapbooking supplies."

I admitted, "You know, Mark, when I'm honest with myself, I don't really want to put the time and energy it takes to put all of these photos into scrapbooks. Each page takes quite a bit of time, and I'd rather be doing other things right now."

"Like sorting the pictures into boxes and then having them available to be enjoyed?" Mark asked.

"Exactly," I told him. "And listening to the music my son and his band will create while playing in this garage. I haven't wanted to admit that I really don't enjoy scrapbooking anymore. But I couldn't think of another way to achieve what I wanted."

I stood for a moment wondering what I would do with the supplies. I said, "I've got a couple of friends who I met at the scrapbooking classes. They are still into this and would be absolutely delighted *if I asked them to come over and get whatever they'd like. My garage would be cleared out in no time!"*

*Mark inquired, "What is your story now?"*

*"I am a generous woman who has an abundance of time to spend with her family and friends," I answered.*

*Mark laughed. "I'm so glad for you, Stacie. You're no longer a slave to your clutter."*

You can experience the same kind of liberation that Stacie did. She no longer needs to use clutter to cover up her disappointment and frustration. You won't need to use your collection of unused and inaccessible items to hide the truth from yourself either. The mounds of this, that, and whatnot will no longer serve a purpose for you. Detach the story from the objects and you will be free to do whatever you'd like with them.

Doesn't that feel great?

## Now What?

Rewriting a story will bring change into your life. If a story involves you alone, you'll need to make peace with yourself. For example, you might have kept sketches from an art class you took in high school with the idea that you would someday become an artist. This dream will not be fulfilled by holding on to pictures you drew years ago. It may be time to let the sketches go and to come to terms with this longing—either by making peace with the fact that your talent will never be developed or by signing up for an art class in the near future.

Some stories involve other people. Stacie had a new sense of joy and expectancy that she wanted to share with her husband and son. As a family, a deeper bond developed as each of their interests were acknowledged and celebrated. Like Stacie, you may find that some of the people in your life are open to conversation and can be approached to talk about the changes occurring in your life.

On the other hand, you may have impacted other people with whom you are not able to communicate. These people have been abusive in the past and may still pose a danger to you. Or they may be people with whom you are not on speaking terms, or people who have passed away. If your story is not easily resolved, we believe talking to someone about the situation is the most effective path to take. If the story is especially difficult, it might be appropriate to get in contact with a therapist.

One way to determine which stories are resolved and which aren't is by observing your body. Do you breathe easily when you think about a particular story, or do you hold your breath? Stories that you hold in your body are usually the ones that hold you back. The stories that are the hardest to tell, and even the ones you may have tried to forget, can keep you stuck in the past. We will not pretend that some stories are easily explored or resolved. If more support is needed, professional therapy or grief counseling may be necessary.

## Practices to Live Out, Follow, or Apply

Complete the sentence, "I am grateful for . . ." List all of the things, people, experiences, and aspects of your life for which you feel grateful. Good things are in store for you today, tomorrow and the next day!

_____

_____

_____

Take a look at your Purpose Poster and identify the images that represent your relationship to wealth and prosperity. Let these images become symbols for you living an abundant life. If there is not at least one image of wealth and prosperity, find one or several in a magazine and paste them to your board. On the back of your Purpose Poster, identify and describe your symbol(s) of abundance. The access to living a more abundant life (on the outside) is identifying the abundance that currently exists on the inside. It's really that simple.

### AFFIRMATIONS

- "Everything I truly need is available to me."

- "There is plenty to go around."

- "There is no limit on happiness."

- "Today, I am grateful for [fill in the blank]."

- "I have faith in me."

# Excuse #2: "That was given to me. I'd feel guilty if I got rid of it."

**H**ilda, a 51-year-old married woman and former paralegal, was moving with her husband from a large house to a much smaller condo. She told us:

*As I packed for the move, I could not bring myself to let go of any of my belongings. I realized I needed help so I called Mark. While we were going through things in my bedroom, he discovered a broken acrylic box that contained an abstract art project that my brother had given me many years ago. It was buried deep in my clothes closet.*

*Mark commented that since it was broken and thrown in the back of my closet, I probably didn't like the art piece and it must not mean that much to me.*

*I was quite offended by the comment. I objected, "This is very important to me! My brother gave it to me. And don't try to make me get rid of it because I won't even consider it. I am sure my brother would never want me to let this go."*

## Misplaced Guilt

There is quite a difference between genuine guilt and the misplaced guilt that can be connected to clutter. Genuine guilt is a signal that we have failed to live up to our values, and usually involves doing or saying something that causes damage to another person. On the other hand, the decision about keeping or releasing a belonging is a matter of personal discretion, not a moral or ethical issue. No moral law has been broken, no ethical wrong has occurred when we decide to sell something we can no longer use at a yard sale or donate something that can be used by someone else. And yet we often act like "guilt" about clearing out clutter is a legitimate rationale for inactivity.

One characteristic of genuine guilt is the option of making amends by taking responsibility for your actions. Acknowledging a wrong can bring about healing in the relationship. In the event that you have, in fact, done something that violates your ethics or has caused harm to someone else, we encourage you to talk to someone about this, someone you can trust to keep your story confidential like a close friend, a counselor, or a spiritual mentor. Together you can explore ways to take responsibility for what you've done and, when appropriate, make amends. Your support person can also provide you with the encouragement needed to follow through with your plan.

The guilt that is associated with clutter is not genuine guilt. Let us repeat. *The guilt that is associated with clutter is not genuine guilt. Nevertheless* misplaced guilt is a powerful emotion that keeps us trapped in an exaggerated sense of obligation or misplaced loyalty, occurring when we are not honest with ourselves or others. In an attempt to appear appreciative for gifts we really don't want or like, we confuse our love for a person with *pretending* to love their gifts.

> ■ ■ ■
> *Misplaced guilt is a powerful emotion that keeps us trapped in an exaggerated sense of obligation.*
> ■ ■ ■

We've found that misplaced guilt is usually connected to unresolved stories about difficult relationships. Misplaced guilt resulting from unresolved relationships often produces clutter—both emotional and physical—in an ever-circular process. Clutter is not an outward expression of the guilt itself, but rather it reveals, in a tangible way, that we have yet to address underlying feelings triggered by the stories we tell about difficult relationships.

In a relationship that is positive and up-to-date, it is possible to talk about a variety of issues. It would certainly be acceptable to say, "Do you mind if I donate the bookshelf you gave me when I was in graduate school? The bookshelf really came in handy back then. But now I'm ready to buy some new ones that match and create a library." In a healthy relationship, the answer would be, "I'm glad I could help you at the time. Feel free to give it away [or give it back or whatever course of action is appropriate]." Seldom is there a reality-based reason for keeping something that is no longer functional, does not match your current décor, or doesn't fit in your new home. When an item does not contribute to your life in the present, there aren't any *real* reasons to keep it.

The Anderson family lost everything in Hurricane Katrina. In the wake of the tragedy they left New Orleans and headed to Los Angeles. Still trying to decide whether to return to New Orleans or stay in California, the Andersons contacted Mark for help. They were drowning in clutter. Mark first went into the kitchen and saw that piled up on every counter, even on top of the stove, were appliances—two microwaves, three blenders, two food processors, at least two of every appliance.

Mark asked them to tell the story of their kitchen and Gail said, "When we had to evacuate New Orleans we grabbed what we could and drove off. We didn't stop until we reached the Pacific Ocean. Since we've always been active in church, we attended a church the first Sunday we were in L.A. It was within walking distance from our hotel. It didn't take long for everyone to know that we were "that family from New Orleans." It was a bit embarrassing to be the center of attention."

At the memory Gail's eyes begin to water.

"Those people were so generous! Before we left the church, one of the elders walked up to us and told us he owned several rentals and that one of his houses had just been vacated. He said, 'Don't worry about the rent. You need some time to figure out your next move. You can live there rent-free for as long as you need.'

"Ken, the kids, and I were blown away! So we ran by the hotel and got what little we had, then headed off to our new house. Word spread through the church and people began bringing over used furniture, bedding, clothing, stuff for the kitchen—everything we needed!

"It was overwhelming. One day we had nothing and the next day we had everything! It really was too much. We have so much stuff now that it's hard to get around the place. But I have such a hard time letting anything go. I know this might be because we lost so much in the flood, but the moment I think about paring down, I feel guilty about giving away anything that was given to us. I don't want the people who gave so generously to feel like we don't appreciate what they've done for us. What if someone drops by and can't find something he or she gave to us?

"My husband confirmed my take on things, 'Gail' he said, 'is so afraid that someone will get their feelings hurt that she won't let any of us sort through this mess. We're ready to buy a place of our own and settle down here. But I do not want to pay a moving company to move all of this stuff. In order for us to move on, and I mean that literally, we've got to find a way to let go of most of this stuff. I feel trapped by all of this.'

"Mark led us, step by step, through his process. I had to confront my fear of hurting people's feelings to be able to create the space needed for us to thrive as a family. With Mark's help, I wrote an open letter to everyone at the church, thanking them for their generosity and giving us the chance to start over. In the letter I said that we had been given more than enough and were now in the place where we could give to others. We had an open house so that people could retrieve what they had given us if they wanted. We let them know that whatever was left over would be sold at a yard sale and the proceeds would be given back to the church's homeless ministry. We honored their gifts to us, and we passed their generosity to others who were in need."

## Report the Facts

Let's go back to Hilda's story.

*Mark asked me to sit down for a moment. He wanted me to describe this art piece in detail. I told him, "It is an acrylic box about the size of a shoebox that contains a piece of linen paper that was suspended by a dowel that ran from side to side. But now the paper has come loose and on one side of the box the acrylic is cracked from top to bottom."*

*"When did your brother give this to you?" Mark asked.*

*I admitted it was thirty-seven years ago.*

If you have an item that triggers a sense of guilt at the thought of releasing it, write down the facts below or in your journal. Just the facts. No embellishment at this point.

_____

_____

_____

## Tell the Story

Hilda continued:

*I always looked up to my older brother. He is four years older than I so he always seemed too far ahead of me in everything. He was a great student, really talented athletically and artistically. He got all of the good genes, I think. I wasn't good at much of anything.*

*I adored him and loved every bit of attention he would give me. When he graduated from high school, he brought home all of the things he had stored in his locker. One of those items was this box. I thought it was so beautiful. My brother caught me looking at it and asked me if I wanted it. I said, "Oh, yes!" He gave it to me and I've had it ever since.*

What is the story of your belonging? What does this item mean to you? Write out the story here or in your journal.

_____

_____

_____

_____

_____

## Identify Your Feelings

We've already recognized that guilt is the primary emotion triggered by this keepsake, but there may be other feelings associated with it as well.

Hilda did not realize how many other feelings she had attached to the box her brother had given her. She told us:

*I always felt inferior to my brother. I never felt like I measured up. I don't know if my parents really felt that way, but somehow I experienced a sense of inadequacy when compared to my brother.*

*Getting this present from him felt so exciting to me. I got a gift from someone special that I admired. I wanted my brother to accept me so badly that I have been afraid to let this go. As long as I have it, I feel like I have my brother's approval.*

Identify the feelings, other than guilt, you experience when you contemplate relinquishing this item. Other feelings will give you clues to the intensity of your combined emotions, and how difficult it has been for you to address the real issues.

_____

_____

_____

## Assess Your Stress

Rate the level of emotional intensity on a 1 to 10 continuum. 10 leaves you immobilized, and on the other extreme, 1 represents no stress at all. As long as your stress level ranges from 1 to 7 our process will be helpful to you. If recalling this story triggers a crisis response, we urge you to find a counselor who can help you resolve your trauma.

Hilda rated her emotional intensity as rather high.

*Well, if I really think about letting this go, I feel pretty overwhelmed with guilt. I just can't do it. So I guess I'd pick a high number like 7 or 8. I am going to keep this. There's no chance that I'll give it up.*

Write down the number that represents your emotional intensity in relation to the object you're holding on to on a sticky note and attach it to the item next to the excuse.

## Be Present to Your Future

Mark continued to work with Hilda and suggested they call her brother and ask him about the art piece. Hilda was surprised by the suggestion.

*I didn't know if I could do it. I'd feel so embarrassed and I thought it would upset my brother if I asked about it. I hadn't spoken to him since the holidays so it felt doubly awkward to call him about his gift. But after some urging on Mark's part, I agreed.*

*I actually started shaking while dialing the phone. Clearly I had a lot of stress associated with this gift. When my brother answered the phone, I sputtered around for a few minutes. I told him that I had treasured his art piece for years and then explained that I was downsizing, and wanted to know how he would feel if I did not take this item to my new home.*

*My brother laughed and said, "Oh, Hilda. That's so sweet of you to care, but quite honestly, I don't even remember the gift you're talking about!"*

*What a relief that was to me! We joked about it for a few more minutes and then got caught up on the news of our families. He said, "You know, Hilda, we need to talk like this more often. It's been great to connect with you today." He assured me that if I found anything else he'd given to me it was fine to toss it out or do whatever I wanted with it. I'll bet my shoulders lifted several inches after that conversation. I certainly gained new energy to tackle the next pile of clutter. With the support of my brother, I was able to lighten my load, literally and emotionally. I smiled at Mark as I dropped the box into the trash.*

It's easy to assume that since we attach a particular meaning or emotion to an item, everyone else does as well. While an object you own might have significance to other people, those people write their own stories. They don't borrow yours. In fact, your friends and family may have no idea how you feel about a gift they have given you. Conversely, you may have no idea what their stories are regarding this item. How you feel about the people in your life—not how you feel about the objects they have given you—is what is of importance.

Look at this from another standpoint. What if the item in question was accidentally damaged or destroyed? Would that hurt your relationship with the person who gave it to you? The bond you have with your sister would not be broken if the teacup she gave you accidentally dropped and broke on the floor. The memories you share with a favorite coworker

*Clutter Confessions*

## Carmen

After my father passed away, I found it extremely difficult to let go of my father's musical instruments. Since I didn't play the trombone or mandolin, I kept them in their cases and stored them in my garage where they gathered dust year after year. Each time I moved, I lugged the instrument boxes to the next house in the false belief that I was somehow honoring my father by keeping his stuff. I heard about a music school in Nepal that desperately needed musical instruments. I dug out my dad's trombone and mandolin and donated them to the school. I am certain that my father would have preferred they be used by students who loved to play, than having them stored, but unused, in my garage.

would not spoil if your roof leaked onto a painting she gave you. If all of your possessions were destroyed by a natural disaster, you would not be blamed for the loss. Nothing can genuinely change the essence of your relationships, certainly not a physical possession. It's when we make a conscious choice to let go of the gift that we start to worry about hurting the other person.

## Sort Your Stories

The stories you've attached to the gifts you've received are your own. It's up to you to accept responsibility for your stories. You have the power to give or take away whatever meaning you choose. You have the capacity to honor your loved ones irrespective of the things they have given you.


In Hilda's case, having a current and honest relationship with her brother was of supreme value to her. Once she and her brother talked more openly, Hilda quickly realized that the feelings of guilt she had attached to the acrylic box, her story or excuse, was keeping her from having those intentions realized. In the end, it wasn't about giving up the box, it was about giving up the misplaced guilt. It was about giving up a story that stood in the way of the relationship she wanted to have with her brother.

Take a look at your "guilty" item and ask yourself the question, "Why do I choose to burden myself with items that trigger emotions that keep me stuck?" There is no reality-based reason. Rather than burden yourself and your home with objects that trigger misplaced guilt, focus on the kind of relationship you'd like to have with the person who gave it to you. Separate the guilt from the item and you'll find the freedom to put your time and energy into strengthening and enhancing your relationships with other people.

Envision the kind of relationships you'd really like to develop with people in your life, and let that vision motivate you to move beyond the guilt to a deeper experience of friendship and love.

## Practices to Live Out, Follow, or Apply

Take a look at your Purpose Poster and see if there is something on there that represents the relationship you would like to have with people, in particular, the person who gave you an item that you no longer need, use, or want, and yet you can't let it go. If there is not one, find an image from a magazine that reflects the relationship you want to have and paste it to your board.

### AFFIRMATIONS

- "I am committed to having open and honest relationships with the people in my life."

- "The most important value I place on relationships is [fill in the blank]."

- "A gift is an expression of love, not love itself."

- "I will properly care for the gifts that are important and relevant to who I am today."

# 10

# Excuse #3: "I've had this since I was a child."

Tiffany and Eddie, both in their mid-twenties, had met in graduate school and had been married less than a year when they called Mark for assistance. Tiffany recounted:

*When Mark arrived, Eddie explained to him that we both wanted to buy a house and start a family. He told Mark, "In order to save money for a down payment, we moved in here with Tiffany's mother. Neither Tiffany nor I had any idea what stress that decision would bring." I couldn't have agreed more.*

*Inviting Mark into the entryway, I told him, "I was actually excited to come back to the neighborhood. Being a close African-American* community, *many of the families have lived in the area for years. In fact, Eddie and I want to buy a place nearby when we can afford it.*"

Eddie and I took Mark on a tour of the three-bedroom, one bath house. Wherever Mark looked he saw at least two, sometimes three, of every item. Two dining room sets with chairs stacked on top of each other were wedged into the breakfast nook, while a third set was pushed against another wall. I explained, "Mom has had that kitchen table since I was a kid and Eddie and I had just bought this new dinette set before we decided to move in here. The one on its side is my grandmother's."

Mark counted three televisions of various sizes and vintages in the family room. Eddie smiled and said, "Can't have too many TVs now, can you?" Even though there was a long sectional sofa, two recliners, and a love seat in the living room, there was no seating available. Every flat surface was buried beneath photo albums, newspapers, books of all varieties, sewing supplies, and unfinished sewing projects. I could tell what Mark was thinking so I said, "My mother loves needlepoint and embroidery."

The overstuffed linen closet in the hall couldn't be closed due to the blankets, sheets, embroidered doilies, and tablecloths spilling out onto the floor. In the bathroom, the stack of towels was so high that it almost touched the ceiling. I pointed out that my mother lived in one bedroom and my grandmother in another, and both rooms were full of additional photo boxes, more linens, and the keepsakes that didn't fit anywhere else.

Mark asked to see the room where Eddie and I were staying. There was one small path that led from the door to the bed as every square inch was taken up by the sum total of our possessions. Sarcastically, Eddie said, "It's so romantic in here."

I observed, "I don't think Eddie knew when we moved in here that he married into three generations of clutter."

*Eddie confessed, "It's really depressing to come home after work and literally have nowhere to sit down. Every time I suggest we have a yard sale to get rid of some of this stuff, I get total resistance. It's three against one." He added, "This isn't the best way to start out a marriage."*

*I told Mark, "As if having four adults trying to live in such a small space wasn't difficult enough, a few months after we moved in, I found out I was expecting. While we are happy about starting a family together, the lack of space and ever-mounting tension in the house is robbing us of the joy of approaching parenthood." Coming full circle on the house tour, we led Mark to the dining room. I told him, "We are going to turn the dining room into a nursery."*

*Too full of furniture to actually walk inside, we stood at the door as I explained, "That pale yellow French provincial dresser and the rocking chair is what I had when I was a baby. My mother wants me to use the crib and matching chest of drawers that she had as an infant, and my grandmother kept the rocking chair that her mother had rocked her in and wants me to use that one as well. We've had more than one argument about this." I pointed to my rocking chair and said, "I remember my dad rocking me in that chair and I can feel his presence sitting there with me. That's pretty much all I have left of him after he moved out when I was in grade school, so I'm pretty determined not to give that up."*

## The Power of Memories

Memories are powerful on so many levels—they can evoke a recollection of past experiences so clear that at times we can almost smell the cookies that once baked in the oven, feel the softness of a pet's fur, or hear the laughter of childhood friends that used to play in the yard. Perhaps the strongest connection we can have with an item is when it reminds us of those we have loved—some we have lost through death and some we may hope to see again. Even though we know intellectually that a memory is kept in our minds and hearts, not in an object, we feel that letting go of the item that we associate with a loved one is akin to being ripped away from that special person.

To work through this process for yourself, we recommend that you select an item with an emotional intensity of level 4 to 5—something to which you've connected a story that has some strength of attachment but that is not overwhelming. It will also be helpful if it were a smaller item that you can pick up and bring into the room where you are reading.

## Report the Facts

Tiffany continues her story:

> *Mark asked me to describe what I saw in front of me. I responded, "I see two rocking chairs, two ottomans, one cradle, four chests of drawers—two of which have matching hutches."*
>
> *"All in one very small room," added Eddie with a smile.*

What are the facts about your item? Perhaps it is a baseball that is grass-stained and a little bit ripped? Did you pick the tarnished pair of scissors that sits in your bathroom drawer? What about the small silver cup that has the initial "R" etched on the side? Describe the item below or in your journal.

_____

_____

_____

## Tell the Story

Next tell the story about the item you chose. For example:

- The tattered baseball was the one your father caught when you two went to see the Dodgers on your fifteenth birthday. You were so proud of him, and delighted when he gave the baseball to you as a reminder of that special day.

- The scissors are the ones that your grandfather used when he worked as a barber. They are a bit tarnished now, but the scissors are good quality and remind you of the man you met only a few times when you were a child.

- Even though "R" is not your family initial, you keep this cup because it reminds you of the times you got to attend antique shows with your best friend's family. You remember being starry-eyed looking at all of the sparkling silver goblets and tableware. The silver cup was so beautiful; you couldn't help but admire it. Your friend's mother saw you looking at the cup and bought it for you. You had never had anything so beautiful before.

Tiffany had memories connected to the baby furniture stuffed into the dining room.

*Mark pointed out to me, "Tiffany, there is a genealogy to this collection of furniture. Your grandmother started the tradition of saving childhood memories by keeping large items of furniture, which was passed down to your mother and then down to you."*

*That made sense.*

*Mark continued, "You are all living out of the same story: Let go of the furniture and you will lose your childhood."*

*"Yes," I said, "I can see that. None of us wants to give up our own childhood memories. That's why there is so much tension in this house. I say that since this is my baby, I should be the one who gets to keep her furniture."*

Write the story of your item here or in your journal.

_____

_____

_____

_____

_____

## Identify Your Feelings

Mark continued to work with Tiffany.

> Mark then asked me, "What message did your mother and grand-mother pass on to you?"
>
> I immediately said, "Strength of family. We are a family of proud African-American women who have had to maintain the importance of family regardless of what came our way." I added, "My grandfather was killed in Korea and my dad left my mom for another woman. Both women raised children on their own, long before anyone coined the phrase, 'single parent.'"
>
> Mark turned to my husband and asked, "Eddie, what do you feel when you look around this house?"
>
> Eddie said, "I feel suffocated. There's no room to live in this house."
>
> I agreed. "I feel stuck. I know we need to be here so that someday we can afford to buy our own place. But in the quest for having a family, it feels like we're sacrificing our marriage. I feel like there's no way out."

What feelings do you experience when thinking about the thing you've kept since you were little? Perhaps the tattered baseball triggers feelings of closeness with your father, and pride in the fact that he was *your* father. The scissors that your grandfather used when he worked as a barber may give you a feeling of connectedness—that you are a part of a family that worked hard. You might also feel a bit nostalgic for an era gone by and sadness that you weren't able to spend much time with him. The cup you've kept might remind you of the times when you were able to get away from the disharmony of your childhood home. You may feel the excitement you did as a child, and gratitude to have been included in this and other experiences you had with your best friend's family.

Identify the feelings you associate with your chosen item.

_____

_____

_____

## Assess Your Stress

Next, Mark asked Tiffany about the stress she was feeling.

> *Mark asked both me and Eddie, "From a scale of 1 to 10, how stressful it this situation for you?"*
>
> *I told him, "For me it's at least a 6 or 7; maybe sometimes when I'm arguing with my mother and grandmother, it moves up to an 8. I don't know what to do about it. Every day it gets harder to deal with."*
>
> *My husband said, "I agree with Tiffany. It's a 7 and rising. I don't know if our marriage can survive this."*

Let's look at the three examples we've been using. What intensity of emotion could be linked to these stories about the past? Perhaps the baseball story is a 3. You might find yourself imagining, "I've been blessed with quite a few good memories of my dad."

The story about the scissors might be a little higher, around the 5 mark. "It's the only thing I have to remind me of my grandfather. This is very meaningful to me."

The teacup story may be a highly charged story: "I used to hate going home after staying with my best friend. My mother drank all the time and yelled at me from the minute I came home. She was really angry that I was given the teacup. She tried to grab it from me, and I knew she'd break it if she could. So I ran to my room and barricaded the door. I hid the cup, knowing that when she sobered up, she'd never remember what had happened." The emotional intensity for this story might be an 8 or 9.

How do you rate the stress factor when you recall the story of your childhood? Where would you place it on the continuum? Write your number on a sticky note and attach it to your item.

## Be Present to Your Future

*Mark continued to question me. "The women in your family rule the roost, right?"*

*I answered, "Definitely. They didn't have husbands to help them through life." All of a sudden something dawned on me. "You know, I think that intensifies their desire to keep their furniture. It is something tangible that tells the world that they succeeded in raising their families."*

*Then Mark asked a significant question. "Is that what you want for your future? What do you want to pass on to your children? Do you want to be the 'ruler of your roost?'"*

*I shook my head and said, "No, I want to have a more*

*contemporary, equal relationship with my husband. I want to teach my child that it's okay to stick up for yourself, but also show them what it is like to have a loving relationship where you share responsibilities."*

*Then he asked a question that hit a chord with me, "Tiffany, where does your husband fit into all of this?"*

*That stopped me cold. I had to be honest and tell him I really didn't know. Mark turned to Eddie and asked him, "Eddie, where do you fit in all of this?"*

*He said candidly, "I don't fit in. That's the problem. No one has asked me what I would like for my child."*

*I stared at Eddie, realizing that was true.*

*Mark smiled, and said, "Well, Eddie, let me be the first to ask you: What do you want?"*

*Without hesitation he answered, "I'd like to be able to build the furniture for my daughter's nursery."*

*I stared at him in amazement. "Eddie, I had no idea! I know that you are a great carpenter, but it never occurred to me that you might want to build something for our daughter."*

## Sort Your Stories

Tiffany continued:

*"Mark, Eddie and I decided to go get some coffee together to give us the opportunity to sort this out a bit more. Once at the restaurant, I said to Eddie, "I want you to know that I am committed to our marriage and will move out of my mom's place if it's the best thing."*

*Eddie said, "Moving out would make life easier right now, but in the long run, I think we'd regret not saving for a house."*

*Mark pointed out that, no matter where we lived, the issue of making space for Eddie in an extended family would still exist. We both knew he was accurate.*

*Mark continued, "Do you want to keep the story the way it is?" Neither of us wanted that.*

*"Do you want to discard the story?" he asked*

*We didn't want that either. I said, "No. It's a good story about survival, about family, about courage and determination."*

*Mark said, "Then you'll need to rewrite the story to make room for Eddie."*

*I nodded. "The story needs to be about a family where everybody has a place. Our family has been led by my grandmother, the matriarch. I don't need to dethrone her or be disrespectful to my mother. But the story is also about a new generation that will have a father."*

*Mark looked back and forth between us. I said, "Okay, Eddie. I will let my mother and grandmother know that you are making the furniture that will go in this room. If they want to keep their nursery furniture, then they'll have to find a place to store it."*

*Eddie smiled widely and put his arm around me. Mark asked, "And what about your furniture, Tiffany?"*

*I told him, "I'm ready to let the dresser and rocking chair go."*

*Eddie shook his head. "Honey, let's keep the rocking chair. That's the one piece of furniture I'd really like to keep."*

*We all sat for a moment letting that sink in. I looked at Eddie and gave out a deep breath that I must have been holding since we first moved in with my mother. Eddie hugged me again. "I'll support you, and be happy to carry all that furniture out myself."*

*We laughed. We knew it wouldn't be easy, but the way was clear now. I can do just about anything when I know it's the right thing to do.*

For the first time, Tiffany made room for her husband—literally and figuratively. Tiffany also heard him for the first time. She had been stuck in the familial conversation, "I have to keep this because it was from my childhood." Tiffany was fighting with her mother and grandmother as if giving up her furniture was paramount to giving up the good memories she had of her past. The very thing she was trying to protect—her family—was being torn apart.

■ ■ ■

*A clear vision of the future can provide the courage and determination needed to make that dream a reality.*

■ ■ ■

Tiffany was ready to rewrite some stories to keep her marriage together. Together, she and Eddie created a future for themselves and their daughter that was compelling, so much so that Tiffany felt capable of telling her mother and grandmother that their furniture would not be used. A clear vision of the future can provide the courage and determination needed to make that dream a reality.

Tiffany cleared a path for her daughter to experience a family with both a mother and father. Mark returned to their home for a baby shower. He was pleased to see that the nursery was finished. Eddie was so proud of the furniture he'd made. He had also gotten a friend of theirs who was an artist to paint a mural of characters taken from Tiffany's favorite childhood storybook. Both Eddie and Tiffany felt respected and honored by one another.

## Practices to Live Out, Follow, or Apply

Do you have difficulty deciding what to do with things you've kept from your childhood? You have the power to separate your memories from the items and make peace with the stories of your childhood. Select another item that was yours when you were a child and move through the six steps of our process:

1. Report the facts: What are the facts—just the facts—about the object?

_____

_____

_____

2. Tell the story.

_____

_____

_____

3. Identify your feelings.

_____

_____

_____

4. Assess your stress and write the number that corresponds to your stress level on a sticky note and place it on the object.

5. Be present to your future.

6. Sort your stories.

Check your Purpose Poster and add a symbol of the future you intend to achieve.

## AFFIRMATIONS

- "I am free from my past."

- "It's time to file my past away and be present to this moment."

- "Memories are designed to empower me, not hold me back."

- "Memories are in my heart, things are in my home."

- "I can consider the past and choose freely, not letting my past choose for me."

# 11

## Excuse #4: "I can't pass up a sale! Look at all the money I'm saving."

Connie, a forty-two-year-old accountant asked Mark to help her redecorate her guest room. She told us:

*I live alone and have a two-bedroom condo. I led Mark into my second bedroom, which was filled with boxes and boxes of shoes. Before I opened the door, I told him that I never let anyone come into my second bedroom. Even my closest friends don't know how many shoes I have. I admitted to him, "I know I have a problem here, but it's really hard for me to pass by a sale."*

*Mark noticed a receipt taped to one of the shoe boxes had last year's date on it. "These look pretty new. In fact, it doesn't look like you have worn these shoes."*

*I admitted that I hadn't—but I was going to—I really was.*

## Filling a Void

Whatever we are doing—whether we are driving by billboards or listening to the radio when on our way to work—we are barraged by the message, "You are not enough, but if you buy _____ [fill in the blank with any item], you will be happy and content." If you try to relax after work and watch a little television, you are once again made to feel inadequate, unattractive, or smelly. The length of TV shows dwindles while advertisers expand their marketing efforts, during and between shows. Plus, with QVC and the Home Shopping Network, you can shop twenty-four hours a day and never leave home.

And don't get us started on the Internet! There you are, minding your own business, trying to check your e-mail and BOING an ad pops up on your screen trying to sell you something. We've noticed that it's often hard to locate the "close" tab. You know, that little X that makes the ad go away. It's nearly impossible to avoid the pressure to buy—buy more, buy often, buy a lot.

Cheered on by a society that is fueled by consumerism and a global economy that depends on our purchasing dollars, it is understandable why many of us have purchased more items than we could ever use or display. Buying what you need and enjoy is not a problem. We run into difficulty when the items we buy don't serve our best interests; rather, they add to the clutter already in our homes.

## *Mark*

I used to buy things to make me look more interesting. I guess I thought that if I owned something cool people would think I was cool (clothes, electronics, original art, etc.). It was as if some mysterious transference took place between me and the item. I laugh thinking about it today. The only thing I attracted (and accumulated) was more stuff, not more personality.

Some people experience an inner emptiness or void. Rather than address this issue through spiritual means, through nurturing loving relationships and gaining clarity of purpose, some people try to fill the emptiness with material possessions. The need to shop, and shop, and shop can be extremely powerful.

## Report the Facts

Connie recalled:

> *Mark moved over some of the shoe boxes so he could sit on the edge of the bed. I grabbed a stool from another room and sat in the doorway. He asked me to describe what I saw around me. I told him, "I see a closet that has five shoe holders filled to capacity. Eight shoes in each makes forty. On the overhead shelf, there are at least..." I tried to count them. "...oh, let's see, nine across and at least four shoe boxes high... there are approximately thirty-six more pairs up there. I can't possibly tell from here how many shoe boxes are stacked on the floor of the closet."*

Mark nodded his head, in disbelief I think, more than anything else. I asked, "Shall I continue?"

"Of course," he replied.

So I did. "It is pretty hard to see any of the furniture in this room because I have more shoes piled up everywhere."

Mark asked, "How many pairs of shoes do you think you have in here?"

I answered, "I've never actually counted them, but I'd say close to five hundred."

Mark said, "You have a lot of shoes."

I said, "Well, in my own defense, I never throw out my shoes. I still have shoes I wore twenty years ago." I paused and smiled. "But yes, Mark, I do have a lot of shoes."

## Clutter Confessions

### Carmen

It took me exactly twenty-two months to complete the adoption of my daughter, Jenee, from Nepal. When I learned that the gestation time for an elephant is also twenty-two months, I felt a kindred spirit with mother elephants. This connection took on the form of collecting "elephant" things—jewelry, figurines, tablecloths and napkins, stuffed animals—you name it, I collected it. I eventually realized that my elephant obsession was actually unexpressed frustration. Putting words to my feelings and coming to terms with the protracted adoption process decreased the impulse to inundate myself with elephants. I've since pared down and kept a small collection.

Of course, shoes are not the only item one could buy in an attempt to fill a sense of emptiness. People over-buy jewelry, camera equipment, DVDs, gardening tools, teacups and saucers, spoons from traveling, T-shirts, reading glasses, scarves . . . anything can be purchased out of an unmet inner need. Some people over-buy collectibles. We've seen homes filled with every collectible imaginable. One woman collected penguin-related items—glass figurines, ornaments, stuffed animals, posters—wherever you looked a penguin stared back at you. Some, like Connie, never intended to display their purchases. But they've bought so many that the items have taken over every available space in their home.

Have you ever felt that your buying was out of control? Have you had a hard time resisting a sale, gleefully talking about the money you "saved?" If so, we encourage you to pick up one of your favorite purchases, something that you buy in bulk, and write down the facts. Ask yourself questions such as:

- Where did I buy this?

- When did I buy this?

- How often do I buy items like this?

_____

_____

_____

## Tell the Story

Like everything else in your home, your purchases have a story. It is possible that you have a separate story for each purchase, but most likely these items, as a group, tell a singular story. It didn't take Connie long to discover the main theme behind her compulsion to buy shoes.

*Mark picked up shoe box after shoe box, pointing out that the majority of shoes had not been worn. He said, "Connie, what is the story of these shoes?"*

*I said, "In my twenties and early thirties, I was thin and, if I say so myself, quite fabulous. I dated a lot and loved to go out dancing late into the night. Then I was in a car accident and was bedridden for nearly four months. It was awful."*

*I told Mark, "I fell into a depression and started eating too much. By the time I was able to go back to work, I had put on nearly thirty pounds. It seems like every year I get a little bigger." I smiled. "But my feet never get larger. I know that some people who put on weight have to move up a size or two. Not me. I can still fit into those dancing shoes, and every other pair that is in this room. Whenever I see a sexy pump or a cute sandal, I buy it."*

So what is the story behind *your* purchases? What motivates you to keep buying? What is the story of your item? What did it represent to you when you first bought it? What does it represent now?

_____

_____

## Identify Your Feelings

Connie continued her story:

> With shoes piled high around us, Mark asked, "How do you feel when buying a new pair of shoes?"
>
> Smiling, I said, "I feel great! New shoes remind me of my 'thinner days' when I felt sexier and more vital. I feel so good at that moment I buy the shoes but..."
>
> Mark pressed, "But what?"
>
> I confessed, "Often by the time I get home that good feeling has faded. I guess that's why I go back and buy more."

Connie bought shoes for the feelings they inspired. For a short time, buying shoes masked the negative feelings she had about herself. However short-lived, those spurts of feeling good kept her fixated on a cycle of "feel bad—buy a pair of shoes; feel good—then feel bad again—buy a pair of shoes," and so on. Connie wondered if there was any way out.

If those of us who have fallen into this trap had a mantra, it would be: "I have therefore I am," or "The more I have, the more I am." We might feel lonely, or like we have lost our way. Perhaps someone important has left through a breakup or, in the case of an empty nest, children did what they were supposed to do—they grew up and started living adult lives. Some people may lose a sense of identity if they are laid off or if a business fails. We've seen people from all walks of life and all ages hurting due to a variety of experiences. And the compulsive shopper buys things in an attempt to fill the void and negate negative feelings.

We all succumb to "retail therapy" now and again. It's tempting to say to yourself, "I'm doing the best I can. I deserve to get a little treat," and then buy something. But be aware of times when you feel entitled to buy more. Ask yourself, "Am I entitled to collect more clutter, or entitled to a home that supports my purpose?"

Not everyone who over-buys consciously intends to keep the items for themselves. We've worked with people who intend to give most of what they buy away—to their children, to their parents, to their friends or to a good cause—but somehow the gifts are not delivered. They pile up inside our homes like toys in Santa's workshop before he sets out on Christmas Eve. Instead of handing these items off to people who really need them, these clutterers hang on to everything they buy in an attempt to meet some need within themselves.

> *Ask yourself, "Am I entitled to collect more clutter, or entitled to a home that supports my purpose?"*

## Assess Your Stress

How intense are the feelings you have when you buy something? Do the relief and joy you experience rate a 3, a 6, an 8?

Now let us ask you this important question: How intense are the feelings you have when you *don't* buy something you want? Where do the feelings of emptiness and loneliness fall on the stress continuum?

Connie told us:

*I rate the intensity of both the feel-good feelings and the letdown at a 7. And there's another feeling I need to rate. I have to admit that buying this many shoes has been an extremely expensive habit. I'm a professional accountant. I know about income and expenditures. The fear I feel sometimes when I realize how much money is tied up in these shoes is very strong—sometimes I feel paralyzed with anxiety.*

Write the number that represents your stress level about your item on a sticky note and attach it to the object.

## Be Present to Your Future

The future can seem bleak, indeed, to a person who can't control their spending. Money slips through their fingers like sand. They are unable to count on themselves to create financial security for the coming days. If you confuse who you are with what you own, you will never find the inner satisfaction you desire.

As silly as it might sound, Connie had difficulty imagining her life without buying shoes. She told us:

*My friends and coworkers comment on my shoes, how many different styles I wear. But I try to keep this under wraps. I know it's excessive. I feel so anxious about all of this. I just don't know what to do.*

*Mark and I left the bedroom and went to sit down at the kitchen table. Mark told me, "Connie, I want you to close your eyes for a moment and breathe deeply. Squeeze your hands into fists and then let them go. Repeat this until you feel relaxed and present."*

*Before long I calmed down. Mark then said to me, "What could you do if you didn't spend any more money on shoes you don't need?"*

*I knew the answer instantly. "I would travel. I love to see new places. I'd ask one or two of my friends to come along and we'd go on a cruise or go somewhere exotic!"*

*Mark pointed out, "Not only would you get to see the world, you would have the opportunity to invest in important friendships."*

*"Yes, I could, couldn't I?" A lightbulb went off in my head. Then I confessed to Mark, "I haven't told anyone else, but the love of my life eventually left me, not because of my weight, but because I wouldn't go on adventures with him. I blamed it on the injuries I sustained in the accident, but I wasn't telling the truth. I tried to live up to an image I had in my mind of what a sexy woman looks like. I didn't feel sexy and I was embarrassed to go anywhere the way I looked. I was afraid that others would notice how unattractive I was and then my boy-friend would notice it, too, and leave me. He got tired of waiting for me to stop being so afraid. I was so afraid I would lose him that I drove him away." Tears came to my eyes. "But, Mark, that was then and this is now."*

Previously in this book we identified the distinction between you and your house, your clutter, your belongings. The separation of identity from possessions is especially critical for those who use objects as a means of filling a spiritual void. We have been encouraged to invest in "stuff" as if it can never be destroyed. But it can be. If you suffer from a natural disaster and lose everything, like so many have due to floods, fires, and earthquakes, you realize that your spiritual being is the only thing that can't be destroyed. It's important to acknowledge that no thing has ever affected who we are as individuals or provided purpose and meaning to our lives.

Don't be fooled by the idea of status or a sense of worth based on things, because it is just an illusion. The greatest opportunity for understanding truth comes when this deception is revealed. Only then will we, or can we, tap into the Inner "U" and find genuine meaning and purpose. Looking for meaning externally prevents us from being alive in the present moment, and it is only in the present moment that we will find our spiritual center.

## Sort Your Stories

Connie was ready to make a change in her life.

> Mark asked me, *"What would you like to do with your story?"*
>
> I said, *"You mean the one where I feel sorry for myself, eat too much, shop every shoe sale and don't have time or means to be with my friends?"*
>
> Mark laughed. *"Yes, that one."*
>
> I said, *"I think I want to release it. There's not much truth in this story. It's based on fear of rejection, a sense of not being enough. I need to fill that void with relationships—with myself and with my friends."*

What do you want to do with the story of your over-buying? Does it need to be released, just the way it is? Or do you need to rewrite it before you make it part of your future? Create a story of victory, not emptiness and loss. Take the time you need to sort through the options and find the right fit for a story that was unable to meet your needs.

## Practices to Live Out, Follow, or Apply

Imagine having an enjoyable time with friends and family. What are you doing? Take note of the emotions this image evokes. How does your body respond? Here or in your journal write out this scene and how it makes you feel.

_____

_____

_____

_____

Realize you don't need things to feel happy or alive. You don't need "things" to be rich. Ask yourself the following questions:

What have I accomplished in my life?

_____

_____

Where in my life do I feel full versus empty?

_____

_____

_____

What if I had a house full of _____ [fill in the blank]? Would I be content? Would I live out my purpose?

_____

_____

_____

What can I do to invite more abundance into my life?

_____

_____

_____

## AFFIRMATIONS

- "The best way to deal with an emotional loss is with an emotional gain."

- "Happiness doesn't come at a price, things do."

- "I choose what I truly need, not a sale."

# 12

## Excuse #5: "This isn't clutter, it's a collection."

Brady and Samantha Weber are well-known collectors. In fact, they first met at an antiques convention. Brady was an exhibitor of vintage magazines, prints, and posters. Samantha was an avid collector of Depression-era glassware. Samantha loved attending shows, picking up a piece or two of glassware, and then wandering through the stalls of antiques. Brady told us:

*I noticed Samantha before she got to my booth. I thought to myself, "That is one attractive lady." I tried to think of something interesting to say to her when she walked on by. Lucky for me, she stopped to thumb through a box of postcards. I didn't hesitate. I went right over to talk to her.*

*Sam asked me if I had any postcards from Cincinnati, her hometown. I scrambled to find anything I had from that part of the country.*

*At first she thought I was trying too hard to sell her postcards. I was trying to sell her on something . . . me!*

*I asked to buy her a cup of coffee and let my business partner, Bob, cover for me for a while. Sam and I hit it off immediately. We talked for hours—and Bob wasn't too happy about that. But Sam and I have been inseparable ever since.*

*Samantha was the one who called Mark for help. At Samantha's house, Mark found himself standing in the entry amidst glassware of all kinds—on shelves, covering her kitchen counters, on the floor, even still in shipping boxes. Samantha had collected hundreds, maybe even a thousand pieces. She told Mark, "Brady and I want to get married in the summer. He lives in a studio apartment, so we plan to live here at my place. But . . ."*

*Mark just nodded. "I understand," Mark said. "There's no room for your dreams to flourish." I laughed and said, "As you can see, Mark, there's no room for me."*

## Collectible-itis

Collecting things is an activity as old as the human race. But it wasn't until capitalism hit its stride in the 1800s that collecting was actively encouraged by the business sector. As early as the 1840s, manufacturers noticed that people liked to collect things. America's love of baseball was combined with commercial interests as businesses printed pictures of beloved baseball players on one side of a card and advertisements on the other. Soon tobacco companies included baseball cards as incentives to purchase cigarettes. By World War I, candy and gum manufacturers had taken over baseball card production and distribution. Today, some of these cards are extremely valuable—at least to collectors.

Just about anything and everything can be collected. All you need are three or more of an item and, violà, you're a collector! Children often collect things found in nature—such as volcanic rocks or seashells. Brady and Samantha collected items originally produced to serve a function; other such items include coins, stamps, toys, or paperback novels.

Perhaps the largest category of collectibles is items that have been produced for the sole purpose of collecting. Manufacturing, selling, and buying "collectibles" is a multibillion-dollar industry—resulting in the creation of movie and cartoon memorabilia (like Star Wars or Disney characters), religious artifacts (crosses, icons, and figurines of saints, gods, and goddesses), dolls from all over the world (Barbies, Japanese geishas, lifelike porcelain), animal figurines (for dog lovers, cat lovers, elephant lovers), stuffed animals (bears, bunnies, and Beanie Babies), inspirational objects (Precious Moments and encouraging quotes printed on every conceivable object), celebrity memorabilia (Elvis or The Beatles)—the list is endless. There is only one reason all of these items are produced: so that we will collect them.

Who hasn't collected something at some point in life? We certainly have—Mark has collected cigar boxes and expensive antiques; Carmen focused on Troll dolls with the crazy hair and anything that had grapes on it. Today all of us are strongly encouraged to collect something, if for no other reason than to assist friends and family in picking out birthday presents they know we'll like. If you're not collecting something, well, you're just not paying attention.

It's fun to collect things, and often we can find others who have the same interest so we can join a community of like-minded individuals. So what's wrong with collecting things? Nothing whatsoever. As with most things in life, it's a matter of degree. Displaying collections in our homes can add dimension and inspiration to our surroundings. However, having our collected items cover every horizontal surface is quite another thing.

## Report the Facts

Sam took over the story:

> *Mark suggested that we find a place to sit down so he could ask us more questions. Brady moved a few boxes and we sat down at the kitchen table. Mark asked me to describe what I saw. I said, "I see gorgeous pieces of glassware, all of which give me joy." I thought that would get me off the hook somehow.*
>
> *Mark smiled and said, "Just the facts, Samantha. Don't embellish."*
>
> *I rolled my eyes and said, "Okay, from the breakfast nook, I can see part of the dining room. I have three large display cases, all of which are filled with glassware. The dining room table is covered with more glass items, as is the floor. Around the kitchen counter is more Depression-era glass." I went on to describe the glass items that filled the kitchen counters. The more I talked, the more I realized how ridiculous it was.*
>
> *Mark must have seen the look on my face because he said, "Don't judge yourself harshly, Samantha. It's true that sometimes the act of describing the size of a collection can be helpful in acknowledging that it has gotten out of control. But that's not my purpose. I want to help you detach these items from the story. So let's take the next step."*

Do you have a collection that is out of control? If so, list the facts of your collection. What is it? Where are the items displayed or stored?

_____

_____

_____

## Tell the Story

Mark asked Sam when she got her first piece of Depression-era glass.

> I told him, "My daughter gave me some gorgeous turquoise and dark purple water glasses for Christmas the year my husband was diagnosed with cancer. While he was sick, I stayed by his side day and night. One night, when he was asleep, I went online to see if I could find any more Depression-era glassware. I was surprised that there were thousands of pieces being sold and traded—a full-blown community of people who collected this kind of glassware. I started off slowly—I'd get a serving dish or a pitcher. My spirits were lifted each time a package came in the mail. Before long, it was my escape, a way to deal with my husband's illness. Once he passed away, I spent all of my free time collecting glass online and going to antique shows."
>
> Mark asked, "How long had you been widowed when you met Brady?"
>
> I told him it had been about four months.
>
> Brady interjected, "I had been divorced for quite a while, but when we met, Sam had lost her husband so recently. I told myself to take things slow." He smiled at me and continued, "But I guess I wasn't too successful at that. I just can't resist this woman's smile."

The difference between a collector and a clutterer is that a collector knows when to pass on a purchase and the clutterer doesn't. If you

■ ■ ■

*The difference between a collector and a clutterer is that a collector knows when to pass on a purchase and the clutterer doesn't.*

■ ■ ■

don't know when to stop, the collection will take on a life of its own. Collecting is no longer about the collection itself, but about a story that has yet to be resolved. You might discover that your experience is similar to Samantha's. She had diverted her attention from her husband's death by immersing herself in collecting. Samantha was discovering that it wasn't her glassware that stood in the way of her relationship with Brady, it was her unfinished grief.

Now it's your turn. Write the story of your collection.

_____

_____

_____

## Identify Your Feelings

Mark, Samantha, and Brady spoke some more and then Mark asked Samantha how she felt about her collection and the story associated with it.

*When Mark asked me to describe what I was feeling, I started to cry. I said, "I don't know why I'm sad all of a sudden. I really do love Brady and want us to be together."*

*Mark said, "No one is doubting your love for Brady. To be honest with you, I don't believe that your tears have anything to do with Brady. I think that you're getting in touch with the grief you've been avoiding."*

*Upon hearing that, I cried even harder. Both Mark and Brady allowed me to cry, without judging me. I caught my breath and then acknowledged, "Yes, Mark. I can feel the sadness welling up inside of me. I think you're right. I've tried to jump over the grief and be back in love with someone else. It's not fair to Brady. It's not fair to my late husband. And it's not fair to me."*

The story of your collection may be about a variety of experiences that trigger a number of emotions—anger, fear, helplessness, sadness, loneliness, and confusion. We believe that clutter collecting is an avoidance technique that works only as long as you keep collecting. The moment you stop collecting clutter, the feelings you've been trying to avoid will resurface. While it might be painful, you have the opportunity to deal with your feelings now—and move past this obstacle. Take the time to identify the different feelings you experience when you imagine putting an end to collecting.

*We believe that clutter collecting is an avoidance technique that works only as long as you keep collecting. The moment you stop collecting clutter, the feelings you've been trying to avoid will resurface.*

## Assess Your Stress

It was apparent to Mark, Brady, and Samantha that the intensity of emotion she was experiencing was high. Samantha said:

*Mark explained the rating continuum and I said, "I think it's a 9 or even a 10. I could burst into tears again, if I let myself."*

Take a few moments and assess the intensity of your feelings. If you rate your stress between 1 and 7, then we encourage you to continue with the practices in this chapter. If you feel that the intensity of your emotions deserves an 8 to 10, then please go to page 257 and read about finding someone who can help you. You deserve the assistance you need.

## Be Present to Your Future

Mark asked, "What do you want for your future, Samantha?"

*Without hesitation I said, "I loved my late husband dearly. And a part of me will always love him and miss him. But I can see a time when the pain subsides and Brady and I will be together. I realize that I need to deal with my feelings, but I have a clear picture of Brady moving in with me. And I can see this house without all of this glassware. After all, I spent the majority of my adult life living in this house before I started collecting. I can see it clearly."*

Take a look at your Purpose Poster and see if you have a clear picture of what your life will look like without all of the items you have collected. It is premature for you to decide what to do with your collectibles—don't worry, we'll cover that in the next section. For now, it is sufficient to create a picture in your mind of a life without the need to buy the next collectible you see.

## Sort Your Stories

Samantha had a major breakthrough, but she still had work to do. It was a lot to take on.

*Mark told me, "You deserve to get the support you need to work through your loss. I suggest you find a grief recovery group or a counselor and talk about what you're feeling."*

*Brady agreed. "Sam, I'll be with you every step of the way. And if we need to postpone the wedding, then that's what we'll do. You are worth the wait."*

*When Brady told me he would support me through this process, I started crying again.*

*Only they weren't tears of grief but of gratitude.*

Samantha had been caught between the pull of the past and her anxiety over moving forward. The interplay of these two forces can result in an inability to act decisively. Even though she loved Brady and wanted to spend her life with him, she knew that she'd have to make room for him. Clearing out physical space was dependent upon Samantha opening up emotional space inside of herself, and altering her life story.

Like Samantha, it is important to embrace the fact that we grow and mature through new circumstances. Even positive changes such as getting a new job or going away to college involve some level of loss. Wherever change is occurring, the need to grieve will be nearby. For example, a new job might require changes in our lives that result in loss. A new job involving a great deal of travel may mean the loss of a regular schedule and missing your daughter's soccer games. A job with strict time constraints may feel like a loss of the flexibility you once had. Starting college, while usually an exciting time in life, can also mean changing residences, maybe even moving out of state, resulting in the loss of familiar surroundings. Some people choose to remain in their comfort zone and reject all forms of change. But it is only through change, and confronting the unknown and also the losses, that we make space for an exciting new future.

## Practices to Live Out, Follow, or Apply

Place a sticky note on three items. They can be different items from one collection or one item from three different collections. Take each sticky note, one by one, off of the item and write out the story attached to that item. If more room is needed, work in your journal.

Once you have written all three stories, examine them and ask yourself, "Do I have three different stories or one overarching story attached to these items?"

Identify which, if any, of the stories are doubly strong—ones that keep you in the past and also indicate a fear of the future. Disconnect the "past" stories from "fear of future" stories, and treat them as two separate stories, rather than one combination story.

You may have quite a few stories now, or only one. Move through our process with each story, until all of the stories you've attached to your collection are sorted.

### AFFIRMATIONS

- "I can strike a balance between my past, present, and future."

- "I lose nothing on the inside by losing things on the outside."

- "No-thing can ever change the way I feel about someone."

Jack, a 55-year-old husband and owner of a home security company, had quite a collection of Beanie Babies—well over 450 of them. He told us:

"It may seem odd for a grown man to collect Beanie Babies, but that's what I did. I had them all over the house—on shelves in the living room, on the bookshelves in the family room, in our bedroom, even in the kitchen.

"After years of asking me to stop adding to my collection, my wife, Brenda, decided she'd reached her breaking point and called Mark. She could no longer put up with running into these little creatures everywhere.

"Brenda and I met Mark at the front door and as we took him around the house, his eyes got bigger and bigger. I guess he couldn't believe what he saw. We sat down in the living room to have some coffee and talk, and eventually Mark asked, 'What is the story about the first Beanie Baby you bought?'

"I told him, 'Caitlin, my daughter, was a preemie and her lungs weren't fully developed when she was born. After we brought her home she had breathing problems and had to return to the hospital. Every time I went to visit her I brought her a Beanie Baby. When she came home from the hospital, of course, the Beanie Babies came with her. After that, I kept buying them for each special occasion.'

"Mark asked me, 'Where is your daughter now?'

"I got a little teary-eyed and said, 'Well, she's nineteen and away in college.'

"Marked asked carefully, 'You gave these Beanie Babies to her, right?' I nodded. Mark continued, 'So how did you end up with them in your possession, all over your house?'

"I didn't get a chance to answer because Brenda jumped in. 'Caitlin loves her father deeply, and wouldn't hurt him for anything in the world. But she wasn't going to take all these Beanie Babies to college with her!' I smiled and Brenda continued. 'To be fair to Jack, this didn't happen overnight. Caitlin would win a spelling bee and her father would get her a Beanie Baby.

She would make the cheerleading squad and he'd get her another one. And it wasn't just for her achievements. When she broke her arm horseback riding, she also got a Beanie Baby. Anything that happened in her life was acknowledged in this way.'

"'Well,' I said defensively, 'she is my little princess.'

"Brenda told Mark, 'Jack has had trouble accepting the fact that Caitlin was growing up. I think he'd prefer if she were always a little girl, living at home. It's been much harder on him for her to go out of state to college than it has been on me.'

"Mark asked, 'Do you know why that is?'

"Brenda answered, 'I talk to her on the phone nearly every day. I don't feel like I've lost her.'

"I said, 'I talk to her, too. But it's not the same as having her here . . . it's just not the same.'

"Mark, Brenda, and I spent all afternoon talking, and Mark helped me separate my love for Caitlin from my attachment to Beanie Babies. It took some time, but I was able to accept the fact that my memories were not inside the Beanie Babies. I saw that love isn't expressed by what I keep from the past, but what I create in the present."

Jack discovered that his collection prevented him from maintaining a close relationship with his daughter. He was stuck in the past, trying to hold on to his little girl and not enjoying a relationship with the young woman Caitlin had become. Many of the people we've worked with who have "collectible-itis" have told us the same thing. Their collections were keeping them from enjoying new experiences, deepening relationships, and fulfilling their life's purpose. You, too, have the opportunity to enjoy the present if you're willing to take a look at the feelings lurking beneath the "excuse."

# Part Three

# Clear the Clutter from the Inside Out

# 13

## Clear Your Clutter with Ease

**D**rumroll, please . . . It's finally time to clear out your clutter!

This is a moment you have, no doubt, been waiting for. We're finally at the point where we are going to concentrate on your home and the clutter itself. As you might anticipate, once a story is processed, the question of what to do with the clutter (that was once connected to the story) almost answers itself. You've already done the hard work of clearing the path on the inside while sitting down. When you stand up with the intent of clearing the path outside, you'll find that the most difficult decisions have already been made.

We have walked you through a six-step process:

1. Report the facts.

2. Tell the story.

3. Identify your feelings.

4. Assess your stress.

5. Be present to your future.

6. Sort your stories.

We didn't tell you that there is a final step—*clear the clutter with ease!*

Some people, when starting this process with us, don't really believe that it could ever be easy to sort through their belongings. In fact, you may still think we are exaggerating our claim. We understand. You've probably heard this promise from so-called organizational experts before. If all you've experienced in the past was frustration and failure, it makes sense to expect to be disappointed again.

But this time is different. It really is.

We are confident that you will find the next and last part of this process to be the easiest of them all. You have an opportunity you've never had before. If you engaged, step by step, in our exercises with sincerity and openness, we believe that you now have the emotional and spiritual space to clear up the clutter in your home—without the angst and drama you have experienced in the past.

You have separated an object from the story attached to that object. Now that this distinction has been made, you cannot look at an item in your home without recognizing that there is a story attributed to it. That awareness, in and of itself, is empowering.

But you've gone even further. You've engaged in a transformational inner process with your Inner "U," that part of you that is authentic and spiritually grounded in the truth. The longings and dreams you have harbored there have been revealed, and you've created a clear vision of what you want for your future. Your purpose has a place in your place.

Lastly, you have sorted your stories and retained them, released them, or rewritten them. The "old" stories no longer have the power to hold you back. The excuses you've made have been identified. You've eliminated any "real reasons" for your clutter. You've exchanged your reasons for results. It's that simple. It's that profound.

Allison had always been devoted to her four children. After her husband left back when the kids were toddlers, she tried to be both mother and father to make up for their loss. Being a successful realtor with flexible hours made it possible for her to be with her children late afternoons and evenings. But she is the first to admit that she and the kids somehow couldn't find time for organizing and cleaning.

Allison told us:

*I hoped Mark had a magic wand to wave over the house and every-thing would be organized. Presto! Magic! I was near exhaustion trying to keep all of the balls in the air. On one hand, I feel like it will take too much time to organize my home. Yet on the other hand, I waste a lot of time searching for my keys and trying to find things my kids need. I confessed to Mark that I've actually gotten into the habit of buying new things simply because I can't locate our existing belongings. And my paperwork is a disaster. I needed professional help!*

*I led Mark around the house that was full of toys, sports equip-ment, clothes, and junk. Lots of junk. I showed him recent pictures of my kids—now 8, 11, 13 and 17.*

*Mark asked, "How do you keep up with their schedules?"*

*I told him, "That's exactly why I called you. I can't keep up. I tried fancy calendars and other planning systems, but they don't seem to work for me. I feel like I'm being smothered in all of this clutter. I sure hope you can help me."*

*Mark said, "I'm sure I can. Let's stand in the family room and tell me what you see."*

*I looked around and said, "I see a total mess."*

*He said, "What do you feel?"*

*That was easy. I told him, "I feel like I've failed my children. And at the same time, I feel like they don't appreciate all I've done for them and won't pitch in. I can't get them to clean up after themselves. I can't possibly straighten up as quickly as they mess up. We're constantly on the go—to their practices, club meetings, and social events. It's impossible."*

*Mark asked if I had gotten the large plastic bins he'd recommended when I set up the appointment with him. I said, "Sure. They are in the kitchen on the floor."*

*Mark said, "Let's bring them in here and label them. Let's tackle the family room first."*

## A Clutter-Free House Starts with Clutter-Free Rooms

A clutter-free house starts with clutter-free rooms. Clutter-free rooms start with the desire. Allison had it. We know you have that desire, too. You wouldn't have made it through this process to the end of this book without longing to live a more organized, effective lifestyle.

Along with desire, energy is required—which you also have. Most people think they have to muster up energy, but that's not necessary. The First Law of Thermodynamics claims that energy isn't created or destroyed. The power to make changes in your life already exists. It's been bottled up inside your unidentified and unresolved stories. Now that your stories are in alignment with each other, and in sync with your Inner "U," this force will be unleashed to organize your home. Energy, when allowed to flow naturally, will help you put one foot in front of the other, not to climb a mountain, but to simply move in the direction of your greatest desires. As you fold your clothes, watch your future unfold. It's almost magical.

When you started this book, you probably thought your house was the biggest problem you had. But now you can see that your home is merely part of the larger picture. Your house contains rooms meant to serve specific functions— bedrooms for sleeping and holding your personal items, kitchens for food preparation, dining rooms for sharing meals, living rooms for, well, living.

■ ■ ■

*As you fold your clothes, watch your future unfold. It's almost magical.*

■ ■ ■

View your house for what it is: a piece of real estate; built of wood and wall board, filled with inanimate objects, with rooms in which to live. Your house isn't alive. It doesn't feel. Your house is a "thing." Only you and your loved ones can make it a home.

The third element requires that you be honest with yourself. Have you *really* done the inner work necessary to separate your story from an item? It can be tempting to fool yourself into thinking that you've adequately reworked a story. Here's a helpful hint. If there is a tendency to procrastinate rather than following through with enthusiasm, then you've probably got some more interior work to do.

Mark led Allison through our process. Allison was able to clearly describe what she wanted for herself and her family.

*I told Mark, "I want to be up-to-date. I feel like we're always late, behind, or just barely making it. I want to be proactive in my life, fully prepared for the challenges of each day. I don't feel like that at all."*

*Mark pointed to the family room and asked, "If this room was clutter-free, what function could it serve you and your family?"*

*I answered, "I'd love to see this room as a place where we all come together and enjoy each other. I'd like to create a space where my children's friends love to come and hang out. I can picture it in my mind—a room full of happy teens, eating, playing games, watching movies, just spending time here. That's what I want."*

## Let's Start Sorting!

You'll need four bins, one large garbage bag, and a permanent marker. If you are sorting items too large to fit into a bin, like furniture or a large collection of things, you can use sticky notes to identify their category.

Label the four bins as follows and include the definitions if that is helpful:

- Retain (items to keep just the way they are).

- Release (items to donate or resell just the way they are) and a garbage bag is for "rubbish" (items you are ready to release that are not fit for keeping, donating, selling, or repurposing).

- Repurpose (items to update or modify in order to use for other purposes).

- Reserve (items you set aside for now after setting a specific deadline to address them).

If these categories sound familiar, it is because they are the same ones we used in Chapter Seven: Sort Your Stories, Not Your Stuff. Sorting your belongings will follow the same process. Let's start by focusing on the items you will keep just the way they are.

## Retain: Items to Keep Just the Way They Are

The items to keep are those that meet *all three* of the requirements of our Passion Pyramid. In order to keep an item just the way it is, it must 1) promote your purpose, 2) propel your present and 3) either be attached to a story that moves you forward, or at the very least detached from memories that keep you stuck.

### 1. PROMOTE YOUR PURPOSE
Allison told us:

> *Mark asked me to look around the room and locate items that my family and I wanted to keep just the way they are. Carefully stepping over the clutter, I said, "I'd like to keep those board games stacked up in the corner." I picked them up and placed them in the proper bin. "And I know my son really likes reading those music magazines, so I'll keep them as well." It didn't take me long to pick out the items that would help create a fun, family-oriented room. But in doing so, I realized that there were only a few items in the room that were worth keeping just the way they were.*

Look at an item or grouping of items and ask yourself, "Does this, just the way it is, contribute to achieving the future I have committed to create?" You may find the answer comes easily in an obvious "yes" or "no." If the answer is yes, then it is something to keep.

Let's say, for example, that one of your commitments is to experience the outdoors with your children on weekend vacations. Be careful to distinguish between daydreams and a purpose you are actively pursuing. If you don't have a trip on the schedule, you might not be as committed to this goal as you think. If you are fully dedicated to creating this experience for your family, then keep the camping equipment that's been hidden away—on one condition—that you have it organized in such a way that, when it's time to go camping, you know exactly where to find everything you will need.

If you're not sure, refer to your Purpose Poster. If the item in question does not contribute to your purpose, then it goes in one of the other categories. You can also ask yourself the following questions to discern whether this item may be of service to your short-term or long-term goals:

- Is this item directly related to what I've said I want to accomplish (such as camping equipment)?

- Does this item add beauty or inspiration to my home that encourages me to pursue my goals (such as a calendar of beautiful campsites or a shell you picked up while camping at the beach last summer)?

- Is it of practical use in living out my purpose (such as a camp guide that gives the current information for making reservations for your next trip)?

If you decide that you do not want to keep an item or group of similar items in their current state, you don't have to decide immediately what to do with them. For now, it is sufficient to know that they belong in one of the other categories.

## 2. PROPEL YOUR PRESENT

A house stuffed full of clutter makes no room for abundance in the present. On average, 25–30 percent of people's households are comprised of clutter. Depending on how cluttered your home is, your percentage may be even higher. With all of the stuff in your house, where would you put opportunity if it knocked on your door? Think of what you could do with 25–30 percent more space. Wouldn't it be great to have space freed up to accommodate new experiences and belongings?

Remember: The goal is not to create a three-dimensional puzzle where every square foot of floor and air space is filled to overflowing. Keep an item, not only if it fits into your space, but if it fits *comfortably*.

*With all of the stuff in your house, where would you put opportunity if it knocked on your door?*

Clothes should not bulge out of closets, drawers should open and close freely, there should be clear paths to every room in your house.

Ask yourself questions such as:

- Does the item reflect who I am today?

- Does it encourage me to live in the moment or dwell in the past or daydream about the future?

- Does this item serve a physical function in my daily life?

- Is it useful to living out my commitment to the future on a daily basis?

- When I think of keeping the item, does my energy increase or decrease?

Let's look at the financial element of abundance. The phrase, "A penny wise but a pound foolish" comes to mind when clutter is a financial drain. The more you have, the more you have to maintain, which will cost you time or money or both. Paying for storage units can add up quickly, begging the question "which would cost less, the cost of storage or the price of replacing these items if you ever actually need them?" Clutter is not free, but highly costly. If it's not relevant right now, let it go.

### 3. MAKE PEACE WITH YOUR PAST

An item you keep just the way it is requires having the space and a place for it *right now*. Not later, not someday. Right now. We've all heard the adage, "A place for everything, and everything in its place." We support this idea wholeheartedly. Consider this: If it doesn't have a place in your home, then it doesn't have a place in your life.

> *If it doesn't have a place in your home, then it doesn't have a place in your life.*

Items you keep must serve a function in your life. The function can be practical, decorative, or inspirational. Every item in your home needs to have a reason for being there . . . or there's no reason for it to be there. Not all stories have to be completely resolved before you can take action; they just need to be current.

## Release: Items to Relinquish Just the Way They Are

We have created a list of our non-negotiables to share with you. It's possible that you have additional or different non-negotiables. Feel free to modify the following listing. A *yes* to any of the following questions means it's time to relinquish the item just the way it is:

1. Is it broken?

2. Is it old and junky?

3. Does is represent a health risk? Is it rusting, cracking, chipping, or splintering?

4. Does it prompt you to tell a story that you are tired of telling?

5. Do you have more than one of the item for no apparent reason?

6. Is it hard to get to or even accessible?

7. Is it out of date with your current likes and dislikes?

8. Is it past its expiration date? Check the label.

9. Did you forget you even had it?

10. Do you have another one that's better?

Allison's experience illustrates that, at times, the best way to deal with the clutter you have gathered around you is to get rid of it. Allison decided to donate the toys her children had outgrown to charity. Many people in Allison's position decide to hold a garage sale to bring in a little money and let other people carry off the clutter. Some items are too outdated or broken to be of use to anyone. Toss them in your garbage bag. Let them go just the way they are.

## Repurpose: Items to be Updated and/or Given a New Function

Allison continued her story:

> Buried in the corner of my family room, beneath a mound of clothes, toys, and sports equipment, Mark found a bookshelf lying on its side. He asked me to tell him the story of the bookcase. I told him, "Oh, I've had that since I graduated from college. Actually my favorite aunt gave it to me. She thought a college graduate should need a place to put books."
>
> We looked at it for a moment and then I said, "Well, I guess I should just toss it out. The paint is all cracked. It is pretty banged up."
>
> Mark said, "I think we can repaint this piece and it would fit nicely in this room. It could serve as a place for the board games to go."
>
> I didn't realize how much that bookcase meant to me until Mark suggested we repurpose it. Over the weekend, my daughter and I stripped off the old paint and stained it. It looks great in the family room now, and it is the perfect size to store the games my kids love to play.

Yes, we want to encourage you to let go of the items that no longer serve you. But we also want to promote your creativity. Before getting rid of a piece of furniture, picture frame, a strip of cloth, or some other item that has lost its original use, think about whether or not it can be updated or altered to be of service in a new way. You might be able to repurpose an item by sewing a slipcover, adding a new coat of paint, or giving it a good cleaning.

## Carmen

I'm a good one for filling bags with clothes to donate and putting them in the garage with the idea of taking them to a thrift store. Then I get busy with my week and forget about the bags, resulting in even more clutter.

Another way of repurposing an item is to recycle it—giving it the chance of a new life with someone else. Include it with your other donations, or set it out at your upcoming yard sale. But a word of caution is in order here. Be careful not to use this category as an excuse to keep items that should be given away. How will you know? If you even remotely hear yourself giving an excuse for keeping it, then you have your answer. It's time to let it go.

## Reserve: Stories You Set Aside for Now After Setting a Specific Deadline to Address Them

Allison and her family enjoyed the new family room they created together. She told us:

> *I invited Mark over for a little celebration—pizza and sodas—to thank him for all the help he had given us. I don't think he noticed, but I always made sure my bedroom door was closed whenever he was here.*
>
> *But by this time I knew I could trust Mark. I asked him to take a look at my bedroom. It was totally disheveled. Clothes on top of every surface and spilling out of drawers. Most of the drawers didn't work anyway. None of the furniture matched. It was a total mess.*

*I didn't wait for Mark to ask about the room's story. I told him, "When my husband left me, I was pretty much a zombie for weeks. I couldn't believe he walked out on me. I couldn't believe he'd leave his children. But I was wrong. He not only left me, he brought a moving van to the house while I was at work and he took a lot of the furniture, including our entire bedroom suite! When I first came home, the house was so torn up I thought we'd been robbed. But then I walked into the bedroom and I knew what had happened. What I have in here now was given to me by concerned friends and family. Nothing matches. Nothing works."*

*I meant to look Mark in the eye and say, "I'm ready to start my life again." But when I saw his concerned face, I burst into tears. I had no idea there was so much sadness inside of me. I sat down on the bed and cried and cried. Mark helped me compose myself before he said, "Allison, the story of this bedroom has not been resolved. You might want to be over your ex-husband, but I sense there are several layers to your grief."*

*I nodded. I knew he was right.*

*Mark continued, "So I encourage you to go see a grief counselor, or maybe attend a support group. Perhaps there is someone at your synagogue who is available to help. When the stories attached to this room are resolved, it will be easy to clear this away for your future."*

Like Allison, you might have items that are stubbornly attached to stories of pain and anguish, harkening back to disturbing experiences and intense emotion. If it seems nearly impossible to distinguish the story from the item, it is a telltale sign that you need additional support to address these issues.

Don't try to force yourself to let go prematurely. It won't work, and you may add more pain to your suffering. Support is available to you. Take advantage of services in your community. And while you are working through these stories, put the belongings attached to these stories in the Reserve pile. Designate an area in your garage or some other space that removes these belongings from your daily life. But don't forget to set a date to address these stories.

We've suggested that one way to resolve a story is to rewrite it. The process might include initially embracing the experience, acknowledging to yourself and to someone else that it really happened. Throughout this book we asked you to assess your stress associated with your clutter. Certain items in your house should have sticky notes with your stress assessment attached to them. The higher the number, the more difficult it may be to deal with the object and the story related to it. Items marked 1 to 3 may be relatively easy to deal with; you probably already know what you are going to do with them. Items marked 4 to 7 may be a bit more challenging, but you should find that you can work through them. For items marked 8 to 10, we suggest that you get assistance. Unlike lower-rated stories, the more difficult stories often have layers and we might be dealing with the shock or aftermath of the event. Sometimes it seems too painful to feel anything at all. When we refuse to feel our own feelings, we might place them elsewhere—such as onto the belongings that remind us of a terrifying experience or someone who hurt us.

If the initial story is disempowering and harmful, a ripple effect can occur. We might not realize that we're upset about the original incident. The impact of a trauma or loss can be diverted or morphed into another problem. An experience can take on a life of its own and, without realizing it, we have created even more distress and disorder in our lives. More hurtful stories are developed and layered onto the actual event.

Just like clutter, layers of stories can be overwhelming and appear like an emotional mountain to climb.

---

## Practices to Live Out, Follow, or Apply

---

Ask yourself the following questions:

- If I could only clear and organize one space, which one would make the biggest difference in my life today?

- If I could only clear and organize two spaces, after the first one, which one would make the next biggest difference in my life today?

- If I could only clear and organize three spaces, after the first two, which one would make the next biggest difference in my life today?

- Once you've identified your hit list of spaces, remind yourself of the purpose each space would fulfill if it were neat and orderly.

### AFFIRMATIONS

- "I am in the perfect place at all times."

- "I am only given what I'm able to receive and when I'm ready for it."

- "I am not alone in my journey. There are many people and resources to support me."

- "I will either have reasons or results. Today, I am committed to results."

# 14

## Strategies

You have gotten plenty of organizational tips in the past—advice given by a so-called expert based on life experience and knowledge. These tips have been rooted in the misconception that your clutter is the problem to be addressed. We, in contrast, believe that unsorted stories are responsible for the clutter. Through our personal experiences, and with the people we work with, we've developed several strategies, defined as a plan that charts a series of calculated steps aimed at an intended outcome.

STRATEGY 1: TAKE BIG STEPS IN SMALL PLACES
Where you used to only see clutter, now you see stories as well. With this new awareness you see bundles of stories and clutter knotted up together. It might feel like your problems have doubled in size! Where would you begin the unraveling of stories or sorting of clutter?

One strategy that will give you the confidence you need to do this (because you really can) is to start in a small place in the room that's on the top of your hit list. Find one manageable area in that room, such as one shelf in your kitchen, that shoe box full of stuff sitting on the floor in your bedroom closet, the end table drawer in the living room, or the stack of magazines in your family room.

- Take a good look at your Purpose Poster. Say to yourself . . . "I know what's best for me. I can do this." Inhale, then exhale. With your four bins labeled "Retain," "Release," "Repurpose," and "Reserve" and garbage bag placed in front of you, sort through the items one by one, placing them in the appropriate bin.

- After you finish sorting the items into their corresponding bin or garbage bag, take the next step. Return the items you are going to keep to their proper places. Items you intend to repurpose can be set aside for now, with a specific date set to address them. Box up the items you plan to donate and put them in your car. Take the items you will sell at a yard sale into the garage for short-term storage. Move items you are reserving for additional assessment in the future to a space where you can store these items. Then stop. Take a break, and take pride in your accomplishment. Leave yourself wanting to do more.

When you are ready, go to another room in your house and repeat this practice.

QUICK STEPS: Big Steps in Small Places

- Identify a small space in any room in your house.

- Hang your Purpose Poster in that space.

- Place your clutter into one of four bins or the garbage bag, then follow through.

- Celebrate your success.

## STRATEGY 2: PICTURE THIS

There is a reason the expression "a picture is worth a thousand words" exists. Because it's true. Our photographs are among our most treasured possessions. People who are evacuating their homes due to an impending natural disaster often grab their picture albums as these seem irreplaceable.

But photos can be of use to you in another way. Take pictures of items that no longer make sense for you to keep, but that you want to remember. For example, the rocking chair, a childhood chest of drawers, an oversized birthday poster with signatures on it, a piano or organ, your first appliance or sofa, etc. Pictures are wonderful because they take up so little space yet can capture memories you treasure.

You may choose to put these photos in an album or frame them for display. But please exercise care when deciding which pictures you want displayed in your home. Choose only those pictures that reflect your life purpose and rejuvenate your spirit.

Pictures can also help you focus on what's important in your life and motivate you to make needed changes. Katie and Randy were living in a house that reflected every décor style under the sun. Katie told us:

*Since Randy is the drummer and I am the lead singer in a successful band, we have plenty of opportunity to buy things when we're on tour. When Mark started working with us, he quickly learned we loved everything! Medieval, Spanish Revival, Mediterranean, Gothic, Post-Modern minimalism—you name it, we had it.*

*In addition to our eclectic tastes, our professional lives were also full of stuff—costumes, equipment, stage props—the list seemed endless. All of this came together to create one colossal mess.*

*Mark asked us a very significant question: "What is your secret passion?" Without hesitation, we both came up with the same answer. We wanted to be out of the limelight so that we could experience a balance in our spiritual lives. We wanted real lives, not make-believe Hollywood lives.*

*He asked who we thought the focus should be directed on. We began naming people who had contributed to our success. Mark asked us to give him pictures of all the people who had contributed to our lives, from childhood on up to adulthood. He suggested that we plan a dinner party to give those people the thanks they deserve. With a joyous occasion to motivate us, we had our house cleared of excess stuff quickly, and without much emotional brouhaha.*

*We turned over 122 pictures to Mark, who had them all framed, some individually and some in groups. We revealed our first ever Tribute Wall at a special dinner for friends and family who appeared in the photos. To this day, the Tribute Wall—which lines a hallway in our home—reminds us of who we are. Focusing our gratitude on other people has brought us an incredible sense of peace and has resulted in a home that serves as a true haven from the lights and drama of the entertainment world. The best part is that we have several empty frames hung up on the wall, knowing that in the future, these frames will be filled with pictures of new friends we have welcomed into our lives and home.*

- Take a picture of items you no longer use but occupy valuable space.

- Contact a local charity and arrange a pickup or place in your car for drop-off.

- Place the picture in a photo book or display proudly.

- Celebrate your success.

## STRATEGY 3: PUT YOUR MONEY WHERE YOUR MOUTH IS

Look around your home and ask yourself, "If I had all of the money I have spent on these things, would I still buy them?" This question will bring you to the present and help you get current on what you actually value in your space based on finances alone.

Taking an honest look at the finances of clutter helped Olivia, a fifth-grade teacher, make some important decisions. She told us:

> I was really ambivalent about parting with some of my things, even though I was committed to creating space and order out of a home crowded with everything I'd ever owned. I did not get rid of anything, so my whole life was strewn around the house.
>
> Mark suggested I do an exercise. I was to put a sticky note on everything I would not buy if I had it all to do over again. I discovered that I had quite a number of things that I would not buy now. I rather compulsively buy products advertised on TV that seem so critical to my life when I dial the phone and give them my credit card information.

*But I would not buy those products in the light of day. I have exer-*
*cise equipment, cosmetics, hooks to put up pictures, and all sorts of*
*gadgets. This exercise helped me realize that my clutter problem was*
*extremely expensive.*

You might discover the same thing as Olivia. Put a sticky note on everything in your house you would not buy again, if given the chance. Since money can be an important factor in the household equation, it's always eye-opening to see what indeed you would buy again. Surprisingly, so few things in someone's house would land in someone's shopping cart today. It might have seemed like a good idea or value at the time, but that time has passed. And now, it's costing more to house it (both financially and emotionally) than it's worth. It's time to use it or lose it.

Cleaning up now will be easy. Simply pick up all of the items that have sticky notes attached and take them out of your house. Donate them to charity, sell them, or gift them to someone who can truly benefit from them now that you've discovered that they are of no use to you, and do not contribute to your future.

We suspect that you will be amazed at how many things taking up space in your home give you nothing in return. The way to truly honor the value of an item is to place it in the hands of the person who genuinely needs it.

### QUICK STEPS: Put Your Money Where Your Mouth Is

- Hang your Purpose Poster in a room of your choice.

- Grab a pack of stickies and start tagging things you would never buy again.

- Collect the items with stickies then donate them.

- Place donation receipt in file for next year's taxes so that you can take the write-off.

- Celebrate your success.

STRATEGY 4: RETOOLING YOUR TOYS

Billions of dollars are spent every year on toys. Some are educational. Some are just for fun. Having an abundance of toys is not inherently negative. But it has its pitfalls. We may unwittingly teach our children to overly value material possessions. Plus, since most toys are geared for specific age groups, within a few months or a year kids can outgrow them. Unused toys clutter houses all over America due to this one factor. They are no longer appropriate for the age of your child.

How you deal with toys that have lost their appeal or impact serves as a learning experience for your children—not just regarding material-ism, but confronting clutter (something we think is important). Toys are a wonderful tool in which to teach kids the power of regifting. At regular intervals, ask your child to sort through the toys to identify those that your child no longer plays with. Some may be broken and of no use to anyone. But most of the time, children outgrow their toys long before the toys cease to function. Toys that are in good shape can be given to other children, donated to your church's youth program or a local school.

As a parent, you have a sense of when your child is able to make this distinction. If you introduce the idea of releasing some toys and your child is resistant, we recommend that you wait until the time when your child is ready. The exercise will not be effective if your child feels like you are taking away beloved possessions. Participating in this experience gives your child the opportunity to detach from material things, a skill you can now model for your child. Children learn at an early age the importance of a charitable heart.

Darcy and her husband, Rich, had three children, two boys in grade school and a four-year-old daughter. The boys were quite athletic so most of their toys were sports related. Truth be told, Darcy had always wanted a daughter and was thrilled when she gave birth to Kendra. Over the past six years, Darcy had bought hundreds of toys for her little girl. Darcy told us:

> *I just can't resist all these cute girly things—I've gotten her a playhouse with the cutest little furniture and miniature utensils, games, puzzles, princess outfits and accessories—you name it. Kendra has it.*
>
> *My husband called Mark because he was tired of tripping over all of the toys. Combined, our kids had several hundred toys lying around the house. With Mark's help, I agreed to give up all but fifty toys per child. I didn't quite know how to tell Kendra about my decision. I was afraid she would go through separation anxiety or feel like the rug was arbitrarily pulled out from under her.*
>
> *I sat down with Kendra and said that I thought we might give some of her toys to children who didn't have as many as she did. I asked her how many toys she would like to keep. She said, "Twenty."*
>
> *I sat there in shock, thinking to myself, "She doesn't really understand how many twenty is." While I sat there, Kendra got up and selected twenty toys she wanted to keep. Took her all of five minutes. I was stunned. I realized that Kendra wasn't nearly as attached to her toys as I was.*

*Mark suggested that in order to complete the process of letting go, for me as well as Kendra, we wrap each toy and give it to a local home for girls. We drove to the home together, and Kendra was very excited to see where her toys were going to live.*

Children can learn to give to others by practicing from an early age. A lesson can be made out of anything a child grows out of . . . furniture, clothes, sports equipment, games. You, as a parent, had the joy of giving to your child. Why not give your child the same opportunity to experience the pleasure of giving to others? Perhaps just as important, you will teach the next generation the lessons you are learning right now from this book—to know the difference between things and people and to create stories about their belongings that ultimately concludes in giving them away. It's important to let the child actually give the toys to the person receiving them. This way, they can *process* the process.

## QUICK STEPS: Retooling Your Toys

- Tell your child it's time to give away some of his or her unused toys to another child who would really like them.

- We recommend picking the number of toys that corresponds to their age.

- Let your child collect the items and help load the car.

- Let your child hand deliver the items to local kids in need.

- Celebrate your child's success.

## STRATEGY 5: SIZE UP AND DOWN YOUR WARDROBE

One of the biggest challenges we have found in our work is helping people let go of clothes that are no longer in style, are showing signs of wear, or that they hope to wear again "one day." Clothing is both personal and public, used to express what we value and who we are. Ever hear the phrase, "Clothes make the man?" Our society places a great deal of importance on fashion as a defining statement of self.

Not only are we supposed to wear the "right" things, we are pressured to fit into the "right" sizes. Beauty is often defined by our size, with an exorbitant value placed on being thin. We've all had to deal with it. If you want to know how effectively you are handling the pressure to be thin, just take a look at your closet. Hanging in your closet, and possibly crumpled on the floor, are the stories of your relationship with food, dieting, and self-esteem. It's time to size up your wardrobe.

An accountant named Jenny needed Mark's help to tackle her closet. She told us:

> *Even though I called Mark to help me deal with my overstuffed closets, I was really embarrassed when he actually came into my bedroom. Every closet and storage space held clothes, shoes, belts, handbags, scarves—you name it. If I could wear it, I had bought it.*
>
> *Mark noticed that the clothes hanging in the closets ranged from size 8 to a size 18. He asked me, "What size do you wear right now?" I told him that I was currently wearing a size 16. Locating a beautiful black dress in a size 8, Mark asked me, "Did you used to fit into this dress?"*

*I nodded. I explained, "Ever since I started gaining weight when my kids were born, I've steadily put on weight. I used to work out before I became a mother, but now I feel too busy. The weight just keeps increasing.*

*Mark wondered if my job was stressful. I said, "Oh yes! After work, when I'm really stressed out, I grab the kids and we head for the mall. We grab a quick bite to eat and then shop the sales."*

*Mark asked, "How do you afford these expenditures?"*

*I admitted, "If there's not enough in my checking account, I charge it. I've gotten myself into a lot of debt. It's ironic. Even though I account for other people's money all day, I still have trouble managing my own."*

*Mark said, "I've worked with people whose clutter consists primarily of clothing. I've noticed that some people keep clothing that is too small for them in hopes that someday they'll lose weight again. Does that description fit you?"*

*"Bull's-eye," I told Mark. "Not only do I buy new things continuously, I keep everything I've ever worn. Especially the smaller sizes. I tell myself that having small sizes, like that cute little size 8 cocktail dress, will motivate me to lose weight. But I don't know that I'll ever be that thin again."*

Mark led Jenny through the steps of our program. She saw that keeping clothes that no longer fit her had the opposite effect than she wanted—her motivation was sapped when she looked at these clothes. They were painful reminders of her accident and self-proclaimed failure in managing her weight.

Jenny addressed her stories, finally coming to terms with the circumstances of her life. She realized that the only way to regain her power and motivate herself to make needed changes in her lifestyle required regaining the balance between her inner and outer space. She told us:

*I realized that the place to start was in a realistic view of my world. With Mark's support and guidance, I decided to keep the clothes that were in my present size, one size up and one size down. I only kept size 14s, 16s, and 18s. That sure cleared out a lot of closet space!*

*I'll admit that at first it wasn't easy to let those cute little outfits go. But to my surprise, I experienced a huge sense of relief when I took them all to a consignment shop. I do have good taste, so they should bring in some good money. I've decided to use the money I get from those clothes to pay down some of my credit card debt. I'm heading in a new direction and it feels great.*

*When Mark checked in with me several months later to see how I was doing—with my wardrobe, my weight, and my clutter—I told him, "I am really pleased with myself. I'm more honest with myself than I used to be. The clothes I gave up were out of style. Except for a couple of classic dresses, I wouldn't wear those clothes today even if I could fit into them.*

*"Without all the pressure I used to put on myself, I'm finding it easier to manage my eating. I'm not in any hurry to lose weight, but my size 16s are feeling a little loose. The kids and I still go to the mall after work, but we try to walk around at a quicker pace and get some exercise.*

*Mark commented, "Jenny, you sound so much more . . ."*

*"Confident?" I asked. "I am. I know I can do this. I'll be able to fit*

*into my 14s pretty soon and that feels good. When I start wearing my 14s, I'm going to let go of the size 18 clothing and give myself permission to buy some clothes in size 12. I think that I'll stop there, or maybe lose more weight until I can fit into size 10. But I don't need to aim for being itsy-bitsy anymore. I feel good about myself right now . . . not someday when I'm a smaller size."*

We suspect that a lot of women and men can identify with Jenny's experience. Envision the doors of your closets as entryways into a new phase of your life. Separate your stories of discouragement from the items of clothing, and write a new story for yourself. Try on the strategy of keeping one size up, one size down, and the size you currently wear. You will find this approach to be the perfect fit.

## QUICK STEPS: Size Up and Down Your Wardrobe

- Hang your Purpose Poster in your bedroom.

- Determine your current size today—not tomorrow, today.

- Go through every item in your wardrobe saving only your current size, one size up, and one size down.

- Bag everything else and deliver to a local men's or women's shelter or charity.

- For all hanging clothes within your size range, return them to your closet with the hanger hook facing inward. Once you wear the item, return it to your closet with the hanger hook facing toward you.

- In ninety days, remove all items that continue to hang with the hook facing inward. These are clothes you haven't worn in three months.

- Celebrate your success.


## STRATEGY 6: FIRED UP!

One of the questions we always asks a homeowner or client is, "If your house were burning down, what's the one thing you would grab?" You might be amazed at some of the answers we get—everything from the large flat-screen TV to someone's first wisdom tooth. The way each of us answers this question reveals what we truly value. The first response is often the most authentic—a reaction to your concrete things versus a conceptual, story-based reaction.

For one family Mark worked with, this question was not merely an exercise—it was reality. The Gladstone family tragically lost their entire house in a fire when the children were in junior high school. More than ten years later, Judy and Bob, and their twins, Jake and Julia, aged 21, were living in a home that was so full of stuff that they could hardly step into the front door without stepping on something. Jake and Julia initiated the call to Mark, no longer willing to live this way. Every room was piled high with old, mismatched pieces of furniture, unopened boxes full of knickknacks, the list goes on and on. It was astonishing to see so much stuff crammed into a beautiful 3,000 square-foot home. Mark literally could not tell whether the living room floor was hardwood or carpet.

Judy recalled:

*Mark sat us all down in the living room. Or rather, we sat on the clutter that was sitting on the chairs. Mark knows how to ask questions* that get to the heart of the matter. Before long he knew that Bob and I hadn't been getting along. We had been sleeping in separate bedrooms at the time. The twins were no longer able to bring friends over. Jake told Mark, "I'm just too embarrassed for any of my friends to see this place."

Julia chimed in, "I've been dating my boyfriend for three years and I've never let him set foot in this house. The only place we've socialized with my family is at local restaurants. It's pretty weird, actually."

Jake said, "Well, let's face it. The house might burn down again tomorrow, so why bother cleaning it up now?"

"Burn down again?" Mark asked. "Your house has burned down before?"

Bob explained that about ten years ago the house we lived in at the time was destroyed by a fire. He told Mark how the fire started from a small spark from a space heater late one night, and how we were all able to escape safely, even our dog. We stood outside huddled together, more out of shock than the cold, and watched everything we had go up in smoke. Bob had the presence of mind to grab one photo album as we raced through the den and through the sliding glass doors. But other than that small memento of our past, everything was lost.

Switching gears, Mark asked us, "What, if anything, have you gained as a result of the fire?" That question took us off guard and silence filled the room. After a few moments, Bob spoke up and said, "The fire taught us to stop putting an emphasis on things and that what mattered most in life is that we have each other."

"And yet," Mark pointed out, "you seem to be enslaved by your belongings."

Well, that comment hit home with me and I started to cry. Mark asked me, "When you think back to certain items you lost in the fire, *did losing those items in any way change the love you had for your family?"*

*"Of course not," I said, wiping my eyes.*

*". . . or did it diminish the love you had for the people who gave you those things?"*

*"No," I replied.*

*Mark kept going. "On the flipside, did any of those people love you any differently after the items were gone?"*

*I said emphatically, "No, no, no. Not at all! If anything, quite the opposite."*

*As my words sank in, I teared up again. "Love is not determined by the stuff we have."*

*Mark pointed out, "And yet, the stuff you have now is getting in the way of expressing that love."*

*Bob said, "I guess we've been trying to fill the void left by the fire. I can see that now. All of this clutter is a way to make up for what we lost. But it's not working."*

*Mark said, "I think it's time to rewrite that story."*

It's possible that you have also suffered from a fire, or a natural disaster like a flood or earthquake. Traumatic experiences like these can come with stories that affect us for years, even for a lifetime. But you do not have to allow such an experience to chart your future. You can rewrite this story by working through the steps in our process. We encourage you to do so. You know one thing that those who have never suffered such a loss do not—you know for a certainty what you value and what you don't, what is important to you and what isn't.

- Based on the size of a room, set an egg timer to one, two, or three minutes.

- With a pack of stickies in hand, quickly place a sticky on all the things that you would grab in case of a fire. Very quickly you become present to the things that REALLY matter and also the things that don't.

- Consider reallocating the things that you didn't put stickies on for they may not really be the things you cherish.

## STRATEGY 7: PROJECT INTERRUPTUS

If an unfinished project verbally pestered you on a daily basis, would you tolerate it? They might not talk aloud, but the very sight of them nags at us relentlessly. Unfinished projects remind us of our failures, our lack of time, and ultimately, unfulfilled desires. They tell us every day that we are not living up to our potential, yet we keep them around in hopes of *one day....*

A garden that hasn't been touched in months, a broken down washing machine that has yet to be repaired and sold, boxes of laminate flooring that will one day go in the bedroom. Software or training tapes to start a new business, gallons of paint for sprucing up the guest bedroom, or car parts for repairing the '67 Corvette that have been sitting in the garage for eight years. Whew! Unfinished projects are everywhere.

Here's the catch! The real interruption is not to the project, but to your life—and it's happening day after day after day. How can you continue on your path of purpose when you are constantly being interrupted by these disempowering stories?

We encourage you to not only get rid of projects in your life that aren't active, but to limit the number of active projects in your life. Our recommendation is based on the 3-2-1 principle:

Three projects that you can complete within a day.

Two projects that you can complete within a week.

One project that you can complete within a month.

Since new projects come up all the time (such as decluttering your home), the first step is to assess how long it will reasonably take to complete it. If you have room on your dance card, then take it on. If not, don't. If you want to take on a new project, trade out one of the projects you've planned to attack. Do your best to keep your "one-day" projects to a realistic number.

> **QUICK STEPS: Project Interruptus**

- Hang your Purpose Poster in the room where you house lots of projects.

- Identify a project at hand and ask yourself, "Am I currently working on it? Is it an active project?"

- If it's not an active project, meaning you haven't touched it or thought about it recently, let it go.

- If you have thought about it or worked on it recently, assess the amount of true time it will take to complete it from this point forward.

- Keep only six projects that support your purpose based upon their individual completion time. Three daily projects, two weekly projects, and one monthly project.

- Recycle, donate, or let go of the others.

- As you complete projects, celebrate your success and rotate as necessary.

## STRATEGY 8: MUSICAL CHARITY

You can tap the energy of a pre-existing source of motivation in your life and use it as a launching pad or companion to de-cluttering: moving to music! There's a reason the exercise industry has produced millions of workout tapes to music. Music motivates people.

Ask yourself, "What artist or style of music sings the songs of my heart?" Is it Gloria Gaynor's "I Will Survive," the soulful sounds of Barry White, the energetic beats of alternative rock, or the melodic notes of easy listening? Whatever it is, put on the music. Once you've gotten energized by the music, get your stickies and start tagging items you can give to charity. Do not stop moving until every charitable item in the space has been tagged and removed, set aside for donation. This is the gift that keeps on giving.

### QUICK STEPS: Musical Charity

- Pick your favorite artist or style of music, one that aligns with the voice of your Inner "U."

- Start clearing space, moving counterclockwise.

- Do not stop until your space is cleared.

- Sort items into your designated bins and follow through until finished with a space.

- Celebrate your success.

## STRATEGY 9: COUNTER-INTUITIVE

If we had it our way, we would post a warning sign at the front of every retail store in America. It would read: CAUTION: PURCHASING OBJECTS AT THIS STORE MAY BE HAZARDOUS TO YOUR HOME.

Truth is, the cluttering process starts at the counter of your favorite retail store. If only we would heed that little voice in our heads that says: "I really don't need this." Instead, the volume of your "I want this!" stories overpowers the situation saying, "This will make me feel good," or "I can't live without this." If you're honest with yourself, you'd probably survive without it.

### QUICK STEPS: Counter-Intuitive

- Create a purpose-driven shopping list and stick to it.

- Make sure everything you buy will have a space to be stored and easily accessed.

- Ask yourself, "What's the worst thing that could happen if I didn't buy this today? Can I live with that?"

## STRATEGY 10: SPACE IS NEVER EMPTY

"Less is more." We've all heard this said before, a phrase that means that the less you have of something, the more you appreciate each item that you do have. From a design standpoint, it's the equivalent of saying that what you don't put into a space is equally as important as what you do. Artists call this negative space. It gives way to positive space and allows you to recognize and appreciate what actually exists.

We'd also like you to consider the opposite: More is less. This phrase means that the more you have, the less you appreciate it. This may sound obvious at first, but if you really think about it, the application of this idea to the things in your house is profound.

Every item in your home occupies space, leaving you with less space to actually live your life. The less space you have on the outside, translates to having less space on the inside. Your passion and zest for life diminishes in cramped spaces. Like a seedling, new ideas and relationships and activities require space to grow, develop, and flourish. The key is to strike a balance between the two and only have things in your house that serve you. At the same time, your belongings, especially your coveted collections, require space around them for people to be able to appreciate them.

If you let the following guidelines inform you at every turn, you will be amazed at the level of appreciation you can experience for your cherished collections. At this point in our conversation, you have the tools to identify the story, excuse or reason for the collection and ultimately choose whether or not it supports you. Once you've gained that clarity, you are free to follow these recommendations for collecting or perhaps paring down:

*Thoughts become things, things become thoughts.* Display your collection in a grouping that says positive and empowering things about who you are, in the present moment. The collection may reflect upon your past, but more important, it resonates with who you are today in a powerful way. Think about your collection. If it's all about the past, with minimal reference to who you are today or the goals you have set for tomorrow, then it's time to reconsider its place in your home.

*The whole is equal to the sum of its* unique *parts.* A collection represents individual items that are unique unto themselves, yet when put together represent a greater message or purpose in your life. Clutter is a number of identical or very similar items that are displayed so close together that it's impossible to see all of the items at the same time.

For example, we met Patricia, a woman who loved to hike and who collected walking canes. She had gathered so many walking canes that they looked like a pile of kindling stashed by the fireplace. By sorting through her stories, Patricia discovered that her motivation to collect walking canes was to communicate her love of adventure and exploring. She was able to relinquish duplicates, thereby creating a collection of canes with a unique set of characteristics and level of craftsmanship and details. Patricia told Mark a few months after she had winnowed down her collection that her friends began to comment on the collection, whereas before no one ever noticed them.

What do your collections say about you? That you are unable to keep yourself from buying every similar item you find? Or that you are an experienced collector who knows how to display a message about who you are and who you strive to be. If you find duplicates in your collection, ask yourself, "How many of the same thing do I really need to express my message? Do I actually need four or five of the same or similar items to communicate something about myself?" A display of unique items of a common theme communicates significantly more clearly than jumbled, squashed items jammed onto a shelf or coffee table.

■ *Remind me again.* Let one specific item remind you of others exactly like it. Instead of collecting the exact same thing, build upon your collection with varieties of the same item.

■ *Properly displayed with room to breathe.* Every item in your collection should be properly displayed and have an amount of free space equal to the space that the item itself occupies. The only way you can truly appreciate each piece in a collection is if it lives next to an empty space that's equal or greater to the space of the item itself. This is a general rule of thumb that not only teaches you to live within your spatial means but will increase your appreciation of each and every item.

■ *Keep it clean.* You should be able to maintain the collection with ease. If having a collection means storing it in the back of a cabinet where you can't even clean it let alone appreciate it, then consider why you are keeping it in the first place. You may discover that there are other reasons you are hanging on to it like wanting to bequeath it to your children or hoping to buy an appropriate display cabinet one day in which to house it. If this is the case, deal with the reason directly instead of hanging on. Give the collection to your children now so they can appreciate it and you can experience the joy of giving it.

■ *Ask yourself, "What difference in my life would one more of these make?"* If the answer to this question is worthy of the space it will consume both internally and externally, the time it will take to maintain it, and the money it will cost to support its existence (including the appropriate portion of your rent or mortgage payment), then by all means, keep it. Just be sure to check in with yourself periodically and stay current with your present-day needs. If somewhere along the way your desire to utilize the space differently arises, consider letting it go.

# 15

## I Wasn't Expecting THAT!

We asked you in the beginning of the book to try on what we had to say as a possibility. Try it on as if you are trying on a hat while retaining the power to choose whether or not you are going to buy the hat or put it back on the rack. What you know now that you may not have known then is that the "hat" is the very simple idea that we are indeed the experts on our own lives, and that following the wisdom within us will take us where we were meant to go. The moment you distinguished the difference between your stories and your clutter, you gained your power back.

The good news is that all of this is a process. The bad news is that all of this is a process. It's good news because your life will continue to unfold as you contribute to those around you. It's bad news if you were hoping that, once your clutter was cleared, you were finished and could sit back and coast. As the clutter goes out, oftentimes the emotions come in. Although you've done your best to address the stories and the emotions tied to your items, you are human after all. Whether it's a small space or an entire house, we've discovered that people can be in one of three places after they've cleared away clutter.

## Inspired and Motivated by the Change

You will remember Regina—she is the retired registered nurse who cooked meals for others in need mentioned in the second chapter. Mark checked in with her a year after they worked together. Regina proudly showed off her organized kitchen. As good as the kitchen looked, Regina's broad smile was even more beautiful. Regina had regained her self-confidence. Mark sat down with her, and asked her a few questions.

> Mark said, "Regina, your kitchen looks great! Is it a more efficient space now that it's in order?"
>
> Regina beamed, "I had no idea how stressful it was for me to cook while my kitchen was such a mess. I can provide nearly twice as many meals to people than before. In this economy, more people need the support I give. I feel all the more affirmed by what I do."
>
> Mark asked, "Has it been hard to keep your kitchen in order?"
>
> Regina answered, "Not nearly as difficult as I expected. When I separated my clutter from my story, I discovered that my self-doubt was rooted in a fairly painful experience. I never knew my father, and my mother was very unstable. As the eldest of five, care of my siblings fell on my shoulders, and I tried to "fix" my mom as well. It didn't matter how hard I tried, I couldn't keep my mother from sinking into deep

*depressions. Without warning, she'd get all fired up and go on shopping binges, wasting what little we got from her disability insurance. She was eventually hospitalized and all of us kids ended up in foster care. I blamed myself. I thought, 'If I could have just been stronger or smarter or something, Mom would be okay and we'd all be together.' I was extremely competent on one hand, but doubted myself relentlessly.*

*"I decided that I could use some counseling to deal with this. I met with a gifted therapist for about six months. Once I recognized that I am neither all-powerful nor totally helpless, I was able to rewrite my story. I realized that I was sabotaging myself by creating clutter in my kitchen. By making meal preparation more difficult, I was punishing myself for not fixing my family. There was a specific turning point— after which getting rid of the clutter was pretty straightforward."*

Creating clutter is a way you unconsciously throw roadblocks in your path for the purpose of impeding your progress. Having these obstacles removed, both on an interior level through addressing your stories and in the exterior by getting rid of your clutter, can leave you feeling lighter and brighter, freer and exuberant. Life just isn't as hard as it was before. Although removing items may have seemed like a Herculean effort, you've discovered that clutter removal was the easy part. The hard part was the process of getting there. Much like the tip of an iceberg that represents only 10 percent of the iceberg's true mass, you couldn't see the rest of the iceberg until now. A balance has been struck between your inner and outer space. A natural feeling of happiness and joy takes over as the voice of your Inner "U" speaks louder and louder. People have reported to us that they feel younger, more vibrant, more optimistic after working through this process.

We have watched people get so connected to the clarity and calm that reside in their Inner "U" that once their space is cleared they take on new careers, new relationships, move to new cities, and pursue goals they had only dreamed about. The list of future possibilities is truly endless because the stories no longer linger and occupy the space. There is nothing better than freedom—the freedom to be you in each and every moment. But not everyone responds like Regina. Having an orderly home is so new, even strange, that some of our clients have become anxious, uncomfortable in their unfamiliar surroundings.

## Anxious and Uncomfortable

Angela, the woman who had buried the grief of her husband's death underneath the clutter, motivated herself to dig through the clutter and uncover her piano. We met with her in a beautiful living room, a far cry from the disarray that existed when Mark last visited. On the piano Angela displayed framed photographs of herself, her children, and her late husband. There was a soothing reverence in the way she acknowledged her husband's memory. She was a woman of purpose.

> Mark asked her if she had started playing the piano again. She said, "Oh yes. But it wasn't as easy as I thought it would be."
>
> "Cleaning up the clutter or playing the piano after such a long time?"
>
> Angela responded, "Both, actually. I had to be willing to start a new phase in life in order to get rid of the mess in this house. But instead of feeling energized as I expected, I'd walk in here and feel

*like it wasn't my home anymore. It was odd, really. I felt like a stranger in my own home. It took a while to get used to a clutter-free environment.*

*"It was also frightening to play in public again. When I was younger, I had a little stage fright. But I enjoyed playing so much that I wasn't self-conscious. But the first time I tried to play at my church, I almost threw up beforehand. I was really anxious. It is getting easier, the more I practice. I'm gaining my self-confidence back. But my reaction took me off guard."*

While Angela expected smooth sailing once the clutter had been cleared, it makes sense that she might feel uncomfortable in a decluttered space. You may respond the same way, too. You've engaged in significant inner work and transformed your interior and exterior space. Even though you might thoroughly enjoy the lack of chaos in your life, you might also miss it. Saying good-bye to a familiar situation, even if that situation has been difficult, is a loss. Transforming a story takes time: Once you've removed the physical reminder of that story, discomfort may set in.

If you experience anxiety or discomfort in your organized home, do not let this throw you for a loop. It's normal and natural. Chances are you've been living with your disempowering story for a long time, maybe even a lifetime. To think that in one fell swoop you can make all those feelings go away would be irresponsible of us to suggest. To the contrary, we expect feelings to arise.

Sometimes we respond best to comparison, so you might want to ask yourself: *How would I feel if I put everything back right now?* If the answer is "better than I feel right now" then we hope that you will be very kind with yourself. Allow yourself to feel whatever emotion is authentically you. Embrace your feelings, even if you feel uncomfortable in new surroundings. Only when you walk through the threshold will you ever experience what's on the other side. Feeling the way you do right now is the equivalent of walking into a new, and perhaps unfamiliar future.

## RESIST THE URGE TO TAKE ACTION:

- Resist the urge to run out and shop. If you need to go out and do something, then reward yourself with an experience. Go to a movie, invite a friend over for dinner, call someone you haven't spoken to in a long time. Someone who would least expect your call.

- Resist the urge to procrastinate. A good way to invite clutter back into your space is through procrastination. We encourage you to tolerate uncomfortable feelings while staying current with your activities. Invite some of your friends over for coffee and enjoy your newly organized space.

- Resist the urge to launch a new collection. After pruning back your collections to a manageable and displayable few, you might be attracted to something new you'd like to collect. We are not instructing you to never, ever collect anything ever again. We're just encouraging you to pause, embrace these difficult feelings, and then once they subside, reconsider if you really want to collect something new.

Give it time and your new space will feel more and more like home with each passing day.

## Regret Over What You've Done

Samantha, the avid collector of Depression-era glassware, told Mark:

> *The process of weeding through my collection was very cathartic. It allowed me to realize that it represented a different period in my life. I didn't need to forget that time just because I was going to get rid of some of the glassware I associated with it. Once I got started, it was fairly easy to select the ones I wanted to keep and pack up the ones I wanted to sell at our next yard sale.*
>
> *But I really had a panic attack when I saw people searching through the glassware, buying glasses and walking away with them. I felt like running after the people and yelling, "Hey! Give them back!" I didn't of course, but at times I question whether it was a good idea to let that glassware go. It took so much effort for me to put that collection together. And a couple of hours for people to buy it all.*

Time and time again, we've all experienced feelings of remorse or regret. We doubt ourselves. We blame ourselves. We fret and revisit the decisions we've made. We both felt that way at one time or another after we've released something we had kept for a long time.

If you also experience feelings of loss and regret, let us remind you that your feelings cannot be addressed by gathering more stuff. You can't fill a void with things. Let's face it, we've all tried that and it just didn't work. The feelings you have when you give an item away or relocate it or repurpose it have nothing to do with the item itself—but may be a signal to revisit the story you had attached to the item. Perhaps the story is in need of further revision. Turn your attention back on your Inner "U" and pursuing the future you have envisioned.

You will notice that as you move through your feelings of remorse or discomfort an inner joy will emerge. Your Inner "U" will communicate and affirm you without a lot of "work." Joy is a natural expression of who you are. As previously mentioned much like learning a recipe for the first time where you have to follow the steps one by one with precision in order for it to turn out right, sooner or later the recipe becomes old hat and you could make it with your eyes closed. That's how making decisions about your current *stuff* and your future *stuff* will become. Easy.

■ ■ ■

*Instead of focusing on getting everything handled in the future, focus on getting a handle on everything in the present.*

■ ■ ■

Once your home is clutter-free, the ongoing challenge is maintaining order. Keeping your home clutter-free is like weight-loss—a daily challenge. One of the biggest misconceptions about clutter is that it takes a monumental effort but that once it's done you will never be cluttered again. Actually, the opposite is true. When you use our method, clearing out the clutter itself is relatively easy. It takes just as much effort to get rid of the clutter as it does to create it. Once you have created a future-oriented home, you'll have to cultivate new habits of maintaining order. By scaling back on the number and size of your belongings, and by having a place for everything and having everything in its place, you won't have to work hard to keep your living space in line with your future goals. Instead of focusing on getting everything handled in the future (which we know is impossible), focus on getting a handle on everything in the present. That's double.

# Practices to Live Out, Follow, or Apply

- This is the perfect time to reach out to a loved one, a trusted friend or family member. You may have spoken to them before about clearing the clutter and this process you are engaged in, but now, it's more important than ever. We want you to share the specific measureable results of what you cleared (i.e., I cleaned out my bedroom closet, etc.) and how it makes you feel. It's not necessary to take people through every detail of your plight. Sharing your success, however, is important to your continued success. And before you end the conversation, share one of your true passions, your true purpose for clearing the clutter.

## AFFIRMATIONS

- "I am in the perfect spot right here, right now."

- "At the first sign that a story is holding me back, I exhale it away and inhale the voice of my Inner 'U.'"

- "I am not alone in my journey. There are many people and resources to support me."

- "Joy attracts joy. Happiness attracts happiness. Freedom attracts freedom—the freedom to be me."

# 16

## There's No Place Like Home

To say "there's no place like home" might sound trivial given the conversations we've had and the time we've spent together. We've talked about your purpose, your passion, and of course, your space. When you started reading this book, you probably thought it was about clutter. But now you know that this journey has been much more than that. Clutter is the means by which your inner truth has been accessed. Decluttering isn't merely getting rid of or organizing your belongings. You have discovered that the

■ ■ ■

*You have discovered that the more you accumulate clutter in your home, the more you distance yourself from you.*

■ ■ ■

more you accumulate clutter in your home, the more you distance yourself from you.

As human beings, we have unlimited capacity to house memories in our hearts and minds. Our houses, on the other hand, are limited by their square footage. If it were possible to compare the enormity of your passions—your gifts and your greatness—to the actual size of a residential space, you would quickly realize the space in your home would be severely inadequate. Your passion would blow out the windows and knock down the doors!

We are genuinely thankful that you took the time to sit with us, to laugh with us, to cry with us. We thoroughly enjoyed taking this journey with you. Having addressed disempowering stories and clearing away the clutter, your home is where you can thrive. The stories that used to hold you back have been retooled and now propel you forward—stories that call you to excellence, stories of your heritage and pride, stories of your passions. What we do with our stories defines our lives and will ultimately give life to our children and their children.

Just like you, we re-envisioned our purpose, reactivated our passions, and reorganized our spaces. It doesn't mean that it's all perfect. But it is in perfect balance. You can have confidence knowing that the quality of your life is improving because the quality and quantity of your empowering stories are improving. The relationship you have with yourself is more important than the relationship you have with things. The more you become successful at home, the more successful you are in life.

From one expert to another, we want to hear from you. We have one final request. At the beginning of the book, we asked you to take pictures of your cluttered space. We now want you to take pictures of the same spaces now that you've cleared them. Print them out and compare the "before" pictures with the "after" photos. It's quite an accomplishment. Congratulations! We're very proud of you.

We'd love to share this experience with you. Please e-mail us or mail us copies of your "before" and "after" pictures along with your story. This book will mean nothing to us unless we can see the fruits of your labor, and thus ours. We can't wait to hear from you and see what our shared journey has accomplished.

We trust that you will discover that home is not just a place to hang your hat, it's a place to rest your soul, rejuvenate your spirit, and fulfill your sacred purpose—whatever *you* choose that to be.

■ ■ ■

*The quality of your life is improving because the quality and quantity of your empowering stories are improving.*

■ ■ ■

# Who Can Help You Resolve a Serious Trauma?

When you look for a counselor, keep this in mind: Simply telling your story to someone else, even if they are compassionate and supportive, will not relieve your stress level. Reliving your trauma will not free you of the negative feelings attached to it. In fact, telling and retelling a distressing story will most likley intensify the negative impact on your life, not improve your situation.

Every time you tell a story that disempowers you, you become more convinced that the story is "true" and you are further disempowered. As a consequence, you will acquire more things you do not really need in order to fulfill that story. Every time you purchase or collect an item that you don't really need, the more you believe in the accuracy of your story—a story that defines you as helpless or broken or victimized. It's a cycle, and having a therapist walk you through this cycle will not help you move forward. You will only achieve mastery over a trauma once you can reframe the story in such a way that it empowers you, protects you, and releases you from the pain.

Not all therapists are trained to effectively deal with trauma. Some therapists are not aware of their limitations and believe themselves to be more able to help you than they are. This is why you need to be informed about your needs and how to select a counselor who can genuinely help you. We recommend that you interview potential therapists, rather than take the first one that comes along. If possible, interview at least three before making a decision. Let them all know that you are meeting with other therapists. Some won't charge you for the meeting and some will.

During the interview, ask what theory and specific techniques they use when dealing with individuals who have suffered from traumatic events. If the therapists seem a little surprised, stumble with their words or say that they will help you tell your story, and that's all they say they will do, then these are not people who will be able to effectively help you. You are looking for someone who is clear, both with themselves and with you, about how they intend to facilitate your healing. Find someone who is trained specifically as a grief counselor, a therapist who works out of a Narrative Therapy perspective, someone trained in EMDR techniques, or other specific treatment options designed for trauma recovery.

Also, observe the way you feel when with them. Do you feel anxious and weak, or hopeful and encouraged? Do they present themselves as "experts" in a way that disempowers you, or do you feel competent and affirmed? A therapist who genuinely understands the disempowering impact of trauma will know that your healing will come as you are empowered to heal. The goal of recovery is empowerment, which cannot be achieved by being disempowered by a therapist. You will come away from therapy even more traumatized.

Remember, *you are the expert on your life*. You have always been the expert, whether you are aware of this fact or not. Being an expert on your life does not mean that you have to face difficult experiences alone. Not at all. We heal from detrimental relationships when we are in a healing relationship. We need each other. And that's a very good thing.

**Mark Brunetz** is one of Los Angeles's top designers and the host of Style Network's *Clean House*.

**Carmen Renee Berry** is a *New York Times* bestselling author, stress management coach, and successful Realtor in the Los Angeles area.

To contact Mark or Carmen, please visit www.MarkBrunetz.com.